DHS CYBERSECURITY: ROLES AND RESPONSIBIL-ITIES TO PROTECT THE NATION'S CRITICAL INFRASTRUCTURE

HEARING

BEFORE THE

COMMITTEE ON HOMELAND SECURITY
HOUSE OF REPRESENTATIVES

ONE HUNDRED THIRTEENTH CONGRESS

FIRST SESSION

MARCH 13, 2013

Serial No. 113–4

Printed for the use of the Committee on Homeland Security

Available via the World Wide Web: http://www.gpo.gov/fdsys/

U.S. GOVERNMENT PRINTING OFFICE

81–458 PDF   WASHINGTON : 2013

For sale by the Superintendent of Documents, U.S. Government Printing Office
Internet: bookstore.gpo.gov   Phone: toll free (866) 512–1800; DC area (202) 512–1800
Fax: (202) 512–2250   Mail: Stop SSOP, Washington, DC 20402–0001

COMMITTEE ON HOMELAND SECURITY

MICHAEL T. MCCAUL, Texas, *Chairman*

LAMAR SMITH, Texas
PETER T. KING, New York
MIKE ROGERS, Alabama
PAUL C. BROUN, Georgia
CANDICE S. MILLER, Michigan, *Vice Chair*
PATRICK MEEHAN, Pennsylvania
JEFF DUNCAN, South Carolina
TOM MARINO, Pennsylvania
JASON CHAFFETZ, Utah
STEVEN M. PALAZZO, Mississippi
LOU BARLETTA, Pennsylvania
CHRIS STEWART, Utah
KEITH J. ROTHFUS, Pennsylvania
RICHARD HUDSON, North Carolina
STEVE DAINES, Montana
SUSAN W. BROOKS, Indiana
SCOTT PERRY, Pennsylvania

BENNIE G. THOMPSON, Mississippi
LORETTA SANCHEZ, California
SHEILA JACKSON LEE, Texas
YVETTE D. CLARKE, New York
BRIAN HIGGINS, New York
CEDRIC L. RICHMOND, Louisiana
WILLIAM R. KEATING, Massachusetts
RON BARBER, Arizona
DONDALD M. PAYNE, JR., New Jersey
BETO O'ROURKE, Texas
TULSI GABBARD, Hawaii
FILEMON VELA, Texas
STEVEN A. HORSFORD, Nevada
ERIC SWALWELL, California

GREG HILL, *Chief of Staff*
MICHAEL GEFFROY, *Deputy Chief of Staff/Chief Counsel*
MICHAEL S. TWINCHEK, *Chief Clerk*
I. LANIER AVANT, *Minority Staff Director*

CONTENTS

DHS CYBERSECURITY: ROLES AND RESPONSIBILITIES TO PROTECT THE NATION'S CRITICAL INFRASTRUCTURE

Wednesday, March 13, 2013

U.S. HOUSE OF REPRESENTATIVES,
COMMITTEE ON HOMELAND SECURITY,
WASHINGTON, DC.

The committee met, pursuant to call, at 10:16 a.m., in Room 311, Cannon House Office Building, Hon. Michael T. McCaul [Chairman of the committee] presiding.

Present: Representatives McCaul, King, Miller, Meehan, Duncan, Marino, Chaffetz, Palazzo, Barletta, Stewart, Rothfus, Hudson, Daines, Brooks, Perry, Thompson, Sanchez, Jackson Lee, Clarke, Richmond, Keating, Barber, Payne, O'Rourke, Gabbard, Vela, Horsford, and Swalwell.

Chairman MCCAUL. The Committee on Homeland Security will come to order. I appreciate everybody's patience. The Ranking Member should be here any minute now. The committee is meeting today to consider the cybersecurity roles and responsibilities of the Department of Homeland Security. I now recognize myself for an opening statement.

I would like to first of all thank our witnesses for testifying today and particularly Deputy Secretary Jane Lute, who is testifying for the Department here today. I also look forward to seeing Secretary Napolitano in the coming weeks to discuss DHS's budget and its plan to maintain operations during these challenging times.

The chart on the screen depicts the roles of each major agency protecting our Nation from cyber attacks. This chart was first presented to me by General Alexander at the NSA. And then separately by Deputy Secretary Jane Lute over at the NCCIC facility. The significance of this agreed-upon relationship to our National security is paramount. Each and every agency depicted understands their roles and responsibilities, working in tandem to keep Americans safe.

The purpose of this hearing is to examine the Department of Homeland Security's role, capabilities, and challenges concerning cybersecurity. There are many issues facing the Department. Today's hearing is an opportunity to focus on the cyber threats facing our homeland and how together we can defend against them.

Cyber attacks come in all forms. America is the victim of cyber espionage. Countries steal our military and intelligence information. There are threats of cyber warfare from terrorists and economic cyber attacks from Iran and from China. These countries are stealing our trade secrets and intellectual property. The most daunting is undoubtedly the cyber threats against our critical infrastructures.

We know that four nations are conducting reconnaissance on our utilities, they are penetrating our gas and water systems, and also our energy grids. If the ability to send a silent attack through our digital networks falls into our enemy's hands, this country could be the victim of a devastating attack.

Yet while threats are imminent, no major cybersecurity legislation has been enacted since 2002. Imagine months without power. An attack on our transformers could cripple our power grids and our economy would follow. This is not science fiction. It is reality. A report recently released by Mandiant confirmed China is the source of nearly 90 percent of cyber attacks against the United States.

Most troubling is that these hackers targeted a company that provides remote access to more than 60 percent of North America's oil and gas pipelines. Hackers have also attacked the servers of our air traffic control system, and just last year an al-Qaeda operative issued a call for "electronic jihad" against the United States comparing our technological vulnerabilities to that of our security before 9/11.

Iran and Russia are some of the world's worst offenders. Last December Iranians attacked the state-owned Saudi Aramco with the goal of stopping Saudi Arabia's oil production. Additionally this year, Iran conducted multiple denial of service attacks on major U.S. banks. The slide up there demonstrates all of the denial of service attacks that have been conducted. You can see it is truly a global phenomenon. It is a global threat.

Unlike 9/11, we have seen the warning signs. But now it is time to act. For us to defend against cyber attacks we must designate roles for all the key agencies. That is DHS, DOD, and the Justice Department. Each play a critical role defending our homeland against cyber threats and none can do it alone.

When DHS was established, the Secretary of DHS was made responsible for coordinating the overall National effort to enhance the protection of our critical infrastructure. The National Infrastructure Protection Plan and the recent Executive Order, solidified DHS's role as the lead Federal agency in protecting domestic, critical infrastructure.

Most importantly, the agencies themselves have agreed that a framework, where DOJ is the lead for investigation, DHS is the lead for protection, and DOD the lead for defense. This would allow each department to concentrate on their core mission with, as General Alexander once said, DHS is the entry point for working with the industry.

In order to fulfill this role, as a civilian command center, DHS has been building its partnership with the private sector and growing its capability as an effective conduit for threat information sharing. DHS manages a bottom-up network of entities from local first responders to Nation-wide threat analysis and emergency response centers like the National Cybersecurity & Communications Integration Center or the NCCIC.

The Department possesses the ability to provide real-time information necessary for instant threat detection and to share emerging threat information to enable industry to act immediately to safeguard critical infrastructure. Additionally DHS has a well-developed Privacy Office to protect Americans' privacy and civil liberties.

While the Department has made great progress, there are areas for further improvement across the board when dealing with cyber threats. Legal barriers, regulatory uncertainty, and a lack of resources remain challenges. Additionally there is not enough private-sector participation in the programs that are already in place because they either don't have the resources, or don't see the value in doing so.

Congress has the ability and the obligation to help fix these problems. For us to thwart attacks we must build upon the Executive branch's efforts and work with all stakeholders to find a consensus necessary to protect this country. As part of this commitment, the Continuing Resolution recently passed by the House includes an increase of $282 million for cybersecurity over fiscal year 2012.

Hearings like the one today will help guide the legislative process. I have made it clear from the first day as Chairman in this Congress, that cybersecurity be the highest legislative priority in this Congress. I look forward to listening to all the witnesses about what works, what doesn't, and what we can do to streamline our cyber defenses.

One of the primary lessons from 9/11 is that only by working together can we detect and deter our enemies. In the wake of that tragedy, the walls prevented agencies from sharing threat information which became very apparent. We cannot allow turf battles to hinder us from developing the defenses necessary to prevent cyber attacks. The threat is real and this time we see it coming.

[The statement of Chairman McCaul follows:]

STATEMENT OF CHAIRMAN MICHAEL T. MCCAUL

MARCH 13, 2013

I would like to thank all of our witnesses for testifying today. Deputy Secretary Lute is testifying for the Department but I look forward to seeing Secretary Napolitano in the coming weeks to discuss DHS' budget and its plan to maintain operations during these challenging times.

The chart on the screen depicts the roles of each major agency protecting our Nation from cyber attacks.

The significance of this agreed-upon relationship to our National security is paramount. Each and every agency depicted understands their roles and responsibilities, working in tandem to keep America safe.

The purpose of this hearing is to examine the Department of Homeland Security's (DHS) role, capabilities, and challenges concerning cybersecurity. There are many issues facing the Department.

Today's hearing is an opportunity to focus on the cyber threats facing our homeland and how together, we can defend against them.

Cyber attacks come in all forms. America is the victim of cyber espionage. Countries steal our military and intelligence information. There are threats of cyber-warfare from terrorists, and economic cyber attacks from Iran and China. These countries are stealing our trade secrets and intellectual property. The most daunting is undoubtedly the cyber threats against our critical infrastructure.

We know that foreign nations are conducting reconnaissance on our utilities—they are penetrating our gas and water systems and also our energy grids—and if the ability to send a silent attack through our digital networks falls into our enemies' hands, this country could be the victim of a devastating attack.

Yet while threats are imminent, no major cybersecurity legislation has been enacted since 2002.

Imagine months without power. An attack on our transformers could cripple our power grids and our economy would follow. This is not science fiction; it is reality. A report recently released by Mandiant confirmed China is the source of nearly 90% of cyber attacks against the United States. Most troubling is that these hackers targeted a company that provides remote access to more than 60% of North America's oil and gas pipelines.

Hackers have also attacked the servers of our Air Traffic Control System, and just last year, an al-Qaeda operative issued a call for "electronic jihad" against the United States—comparing our technological vulnerabilities to that of our security before 9/11.

Iran and Russia are some of the world's worst offenders. Last December, Iranians attacked the state-owned Saudi Aramco, with the goal of stopping Saudi Arabia's oil production. Additionally, this year Iran conducted multiple denial of service attacks on major U.S. banks.

Unlike 9/11, we have seen the warning signs—now it is time to act. For us to defend against cyber attacks we must designate roles for all of the key agencies—

DHS, DoD, and the Justice Department. Each play a crucial role defending our homeland against cyber threats and none can do it alone.

When DHS was established, the Secretary of DHS was made responsible for "coordinating the overall National effort to enhance the protection of our critical infrastructure."

The National Infrastructure Protection Plan (NIPP) and the recent Executive Order solidified DHS' role as the lead Federal agency in protecting domestic critical infrastructure.

Most importantly, the agencies themselves agree that a framework where DOJ is the lead for investigation, DHS is the lead for protection and DoD as the lead for defense would allow each department to concentrate on their core mission with, as General Alexander once said, " . . . DHS as the entry point for working with industry."

In order to fulfill this role as a civilian command center, DHS has been building its partnerships with the private sector and growing its capacity as an effective conduit for threat information sharing. DHS manages a bottom-up network of entities from local first responders to Nation-wide threat analysis and emergency response centers like the National Cybersecurity and Communications Integration Center (NCCIC).

The Department possesses the ability to provide real-time information necessary for instant threat detection, and to share emerging threat information to enable industry to act immediately to safeguard critical infrastructure. Additionally, DHS has a well-developed Privacy Office to protect Americans' privacy and civil liberties.

While the Department has made great progress, there are areas for further improvement across the board when dealing with cyber threats. Legal barriers, regulatory uncertainty and a lack of resources remain challenges. Additionally, there is not enough private-sector participation in the programs that are already in place, because they either don't have the resources or don't see the value in doing so.

Congress has the ability and the obligation to help fix these problems. For us to thwart attacks, we must build upon the Executive branch's efforts and work with all stakeholders to find the consensus necessary to protect this country. As part of this commitment, the Continuing Resolution recently passed by the House includes an increase of $282 million for cybersecurity over fiscal year 2012 levels.

Hearings like the one today will help guide the legislative process. I look forward to listening to all of our witnesses about what works, what doesn't, and what we can do to streamline our cyber defenses.

One of the primary lessons from 9/11 is that only by working together can we detect and deter our enemies. In the wake of that tragedy, the walls preventing agencies from sharing threat information became apparent. We cannot allow turf battles to hinder us from developing the defenses necessary to prevent cyber attacks. The threat is real, and this time we see it coming.

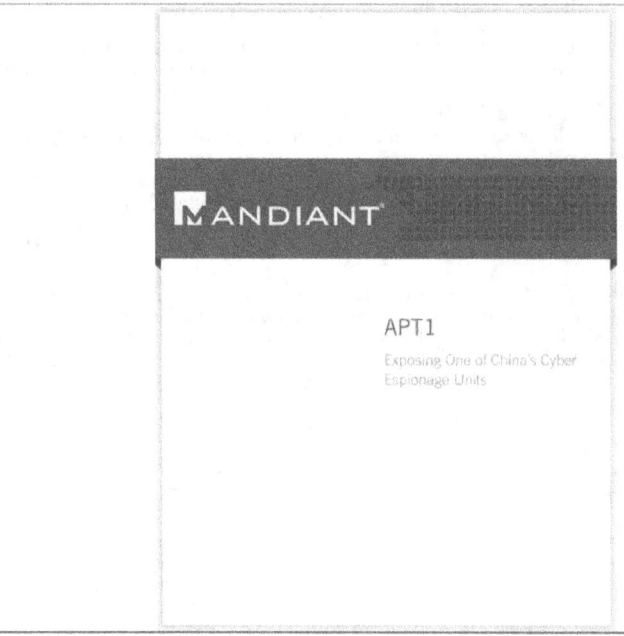

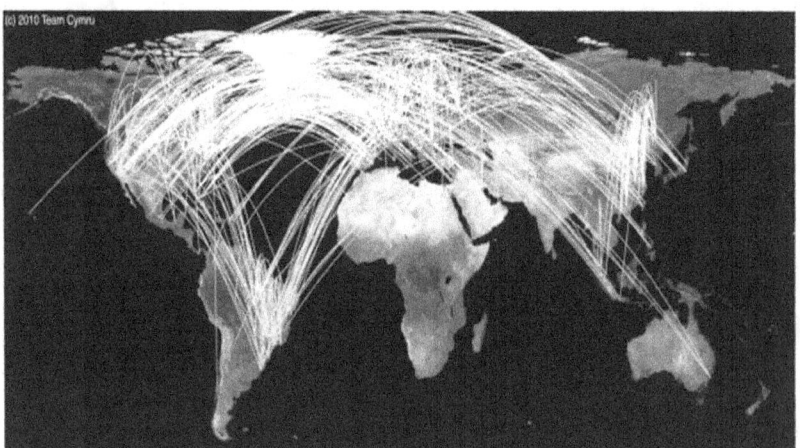

Figure 5: This image shows the origin (C&C server location) and destination of the victim of DDoS attacks for a recent 24 hour period.

Chairman MCCAUL. With that the Chairman now recognizes the Ranking Minority Member, Mr. Thompson.

Mr. THOMPSON. Thank you very much, Mr. Chairman, for holding this very timely hearing today.

Each week brings new reports of cyber breaches. Hackers are becoming more sophisticated. They are hitting Americans where we live, work, and play at an unprecedented rate and in new and very troubling ways.

Last month, President Obama signed an Executive Order improving critical infrastructure cybersecurity that directed the Department of Homeland Security to establish a new voluntary program for critical infrastructure.

The issuance of this Executive Order is a positive step forward. It has the potential to foster unprecedented collaboration between the Federal Government and the private sector on this very difficult homeland security challenge.

I look forward to hearing from you, Deputy Secretary Lute, about the Department's central role under this order, as well as the progress DHS has made in recent years to build its cyber capabilities.

I am also looking forward to hearing from representatives of critical infrastructure sectors that are joining us today about the importance of fostering a close working relationship between industry and the Federal Government.

At my urging, Ms. Richardson of the American Civil Liberties Union is here to help us think about how we can protect that relationship in a way that protects the privacy and civil liberties of all Americans.

While the issuance of the Executive Order is a welcome development, it will take legislative action to fully address cyber threats and vulnerabilities to critical infrastructure.

I appreciate what the Chairman has said about his desire to focus on cybersecurity this Congress. But as we saw in the 112th Congress, simply wanting to pass cybersecurity legislation is not sufficient.

Mr. Chairman, I know you share my desire to authorize DHS's cybersecurity programs and bolster our Nation's ability to ward off attacks to critical infrastructure. However, I am afraid that some of our colleagues in the House have not seen the light.

Hopefully the testimony we receive today will help this committee make the case for moving cybersecurity legislation to the House floor. Even as we begin work on our bill, we must not lose sight of the need to defend, pursue, and exercise our jurisdiction.

Recently, another committee introduced cyber legislation, H.R. 624, which is expected to see action on the House floor in April. That bill, for the first time, would authorize the Department's National cybersecurity and communications integrations center, but the Speaker did not refer the bill to this committee.

Last week, I, along with Ranking Member Clarke, sent you a letter urging you to insist upon a referral of the bill. Our Members deserve the opportunity to consider the Cyber Intelligence Sharing and Protection Act before it goes to the full House.

With that, Mr. Chairman, I ask unanimous consent that our letter to you be inserted into the record.

Chairman McCAUL. Without objection, so ordered.
[The information follows:]

LETTER FROM BENNIE G. THOMPSON AND YVETTE D. CLARKE

MARCH 5, 2013.

The Honorable MICHAEL T. McCAUL,
Chairman, Committee on Homeland Security, H2–176 Ford House Office Building,
U.S. House of Representatives, Washington, DC 20515.

The Honorable PATRICK MEEHAN,
Chairman, Subcommittee on Cybersecurity, Infrastructure Protection, and Security
Technologies, 204 Cannon House Office Building, U.S. House of Representatives,
Washington, DC 20515.

DEAR CHAIRMAN McCAUL AND SUBCOMMITTEE CHAIRMAN MEEHAN: We write regarding H.R. 624, the "Cyber Intelligence Sharing and Protection Act."

As you are aware, H.R. 624 contains numerous provisions within the Rule X, clause 1(j) jurisdiction of the Committee on Homeland Security. Specifically, H.R. 624 contains provisions directing the Department of Homeland Security's National Cybersecurity and Communications Integration Center to integrate and disseminate homeland security information and addressing the Government-wide use of cyber threat information for cybersecurity or the protection of National security. Despite these provisions clearly falling within the Committee's legislative jurisdiction, the Speaker chose not to refer the measure to the committee upon introduction.

On Friday, March, 1, 2013, the Chairman of the Permanent Select Committee on Intelligence, Representative Mike Rogers of Michigan, was quoted as saying that negotiations with the White House on the "Cyber Intelligence Sharing and Protection Act" are underway and that the parties are "very close" to agreeing on the role that the Department of Homeland Security would play to better defend against cyber attacks.[1]

Given that the provisions under discussion with the White House are within the committee's jurisdiction, it is troubling to learn that the leadership of another committee believes it has reached agreement on the parameters of the Department's cybersecurity role.

Like you, we have strong views about the criticality of cybersecurity to the welfare of our Nation, the role of the Department of Homeland Security in that effort, and our committee's obligation to play a central role in shaping cybersecurity policy. That is why we firmly believe that the committee should defend, pursue, and exercise jurisdiction in this area. In light of the Speaker's decision not to refer H.R. 624 to the committee upon introduction, we urge you to insist upon a sequential referral of the measure and afford Members of the committee the opportunity to consider this legislation in an open mark-up session.

By taking these actions early in the 113th Congress, you will demonstrate your commitment to vigorously defending this committee's legislative jurisdiction and protect this committee's position as a central player in the cybersecurity arena. Additionally, it will afford the committee, which has conducted extensive oversight and developed expertise in matters of cybersecurity, an opportunity to debate and inform the bill.

Thank you, in advance, for your attention to this request. Should you or your staff have any questions on this matter, please contact Ms. Rosaline Cohen, Chief Counsel for Legislation of the Committee on Homeland Security[.]

Sincerely,

BENNIE G. THOMPSON,
Ranking Member.

YVETTE D. CLARKE,
Ranking Member, Subcommittee on Cybersecurity, Infrastructure Protection, and
Security Technologies.

Mr. THOMPSON. Before I close, I would note that this hearing is taking place at a time when the effects of arbitrary, across-the-board spending cuts are just beginning to be realized.

I look forward to hearing from you, Deputy Secretary Lute, about how the sequester and the perpetual uncertainty around budgeting

---

[1] "White House, lawmakers resume cybersecurity bill talks," Chicago Tribune at *http://articles.chicagotribune.com/2013-03-01/business/sns-rt-us-usa-cybersecurity-billbre9200w9-20130301_1_cybersecurity-bill-cyber-attacks-rogers.*

impacts DHS's ability to plan, prioritize, and execute its critical cybersecurity mission.

Once again, I would like to thank all of the witnesses for being here today and I look forward to their testimony. I yield back.

[The statement of Ranking Member Thompson follows:]

STATEMENT OF RANKING MEMBER BENNIE G. THOMPSON

MARCH 13, 2013

Each week brings new reports of cyber breaches. Hackers are becoming more sophisticated. They are hitting Americans where we live, work, and play at an unprecedented rate and in new and very troubling ways.

Last month, President Obama signed an Executive Order entitled "Improving Critical Infrastructure Cybersecurity" that directed the Department of Homeland Security to establish a new voluntary program for critical infrastructure.

The issuance of this Executive Order is a positive step forward. It has the potential to foster unprecedented collaboration between the Federal Government and the private sector on this very difficult homeland security challenge.

I look forward to hearing from you, Deputy Secretary Lute, about the Department's central role under this order, as well as the progress DHS has made in recent years to build its cyber capabilities.

I also look forward to hearing from representatives of critical infrastructure sectors that are joining us today about the importance of fostering a close working relationship between industry and Federal Government.

At my urging, Ms. Richardson of the American Civil Liberties Union is here to help us think about how we can structure that relationship in a way that protects the privacy and civil liberties of all Americans.

While the issuance of the Executive Order is a welcome development, it will take legislative action to fully address cyber threats and vulnerabilities to critical infrastructure.

I appreciate what the Chairman has said about his desire to focus on cybersecurity this Congress, but, as we saw in the 112th Congress, simply wanting to pass cybersecurity legislation is not sufficient.

Mr. Chairman, I know you share my desire to authorize DHS's cybersecurity programs and bolster our Nation's ability to ward off attacks to critical infrastructure.

However, I am afraid that some of our colleagues in the House have not seen the light.

Hopefully, the testimony we receive today will help this committee make the case for moving cybersecurity legislation to the House floor.

Even as we begin work on our bill, we must not lose sight of the need to defend, pursue, and exercise our jurisdiction.

Recently, another committee introduced cyber legislation, H.R. 624, which is expected to see action in the House in April. That bill, for the first time, would authorize the Department's "National Cybersecurity and Communications Integration Center" but the Speaker did not refer it to this committee.

Last week, I, along with the Ranking Member Clarke, sent you a letter urging you to insist upon a referral of that bill. Our Members deserve the opportunity to consider the Cyber Intelligence Sharing and Protection Act before it goes to the full House.

Before I close, I would note that this hearing is taking place at a time when the effects of arbitrary, across-the-board spending cuts are just beginning to be realized. I look forward to hearing from you, Deputy Secretary Lute, about how the sequester and the perpetual uncertainty around budgeting impacts DHS' ability to plan, prioritize, and execute its critical cybersecurity mission.

Chairman MCCAUL. I thank the Ranking Member and I also share in your commitment to marking up a cyber bill and getting it on the floor, passed by the House, Senate, and signed into law by the President.

I would also, again, note that, concerning the budget resolution, the House actually included an increase of over $282 million for cybersecurity and I think that is a positive step forward in this mission.

Other Members are reminded that opening statements may be submitted for the record. We are pleased to have two panels of distinguished witnesses.

The first would be the Honorable Jane Lute, deputy secretary of the Department of Homeland Security. Dr. Lute came to this position in 2009 with over 30 years of military and senior executive experience in the United States Government, including service at the United Nations and the National Security Council.

The deputy's full written statement will appear in the record. The Chairman now recognizes Deputy Secretary Lute for 5 minutes for an opening statement.

STATEMENT OF HON. JANE HOLL LUTE, DEPUTY SECRETARY, DEPARTMENT OF HOMELAND SECURITY

Ms. LUTE [continuing]. Ensuring the Nation's cybersecurity is an integral part of the DHS mission, which is to help create a safe, secure, resilient place where the American way of life can thrive.

Four years ago, in the QHSR, the Quadrennial Homeland Security Review commissioned by Congress, we called out five essential missions in order to perform our role: Preventing terrorism, securing our borders, administering and enforcing our immigration laws, building National resilience, and ensuring the Nation's cybersecurity.

Cyberspace has become the very endoskeleton of modern life, and while this connectivity has led to transformations and advances around the world, it has also increased our shared risk.

DHS is responsible for securing unclassified, Federal civilian agency networks and for working with owners and operators of critical infrastructure to help them secure their networks. We coordinate the National response to significant cyber-incidents and create and maintain a common operational picture for cyberspace across the Government.

On a minute-by-minute basis, 24 by 7, our cyber teams confront the dangerous combination—excuse me—of known and unknown cyber vulnerabilities and adversaries across the globe with strong and expanding capabilities.

We face denial-of-service attacks, the theft of valuable trade secrets, intrusions against Government networks, and attempts against the systems that control critical infrastructure.

To protect Federal networks, DHS deploys technology to detect and block cyber intrusions, develop continuous diagnostics and mitigation for agency systems and provide guidance to agencies so that they can protect themselves.

We also work closely with owners and operators of critical infrastructure to strengthen their facilities by sharing risk and threat information through on-site risk assessment, mitigation, and incident response.

DHS is home to the National Cybersecurity & Communications Integration Center, the NCCIC, which many of you have seen, our 'round-the-clock cyber situational awareness and incident response hub.

Over the past 4 years, the NCCIC has responded to nearly half-a-million incidents and released more than 26,000 actionable cybersecurity alerts to public and private-sector partners.

Last year, our U.S. Computer Emergency Readiness Team, US–CERT, resolved approximately 190,000 cyber incidents and issued 7,500 alerts, a 68 percent increase over 2011. Our Industrial Control Systems Cyber Emergency Response Team responded to 177 incidents, while completing 89 site visits and deploying 15 teams to respond to significant private-sector incidents.

We partnered closely with the Departments of Justice and Defense to ensure, as the Chairman said, that a call to one is a call to all, mobilizing all of the resources of the Federal Government in partnership to prevent and respond, when necessary, rapidly to cyber incidents.

While each agency operates within the parameters of its authorities, our overall Federal response to cyber incidents of consequence is coordinated among the three of us. This synchronization ensures that all of our capabilities are brought to bear against cyber threats.

But while our accomplishments our significant, we need the help of Congress, by enacting a suite of comprehensive cybersecurity legislative measures. In the interim, last month the President took the executive action within current authorities and established the Executive Order.

This Executive Order on improving critical infrastructure cybersecurity supports enhanced sharing of cyber threat information with the private sector. It also directs DHS to develop a voluntary program to promote the adoption of a cybersecurity framework for critical infrastructure and to assist the private sector in its implementation.

At the same time, a policy directive on critical infrastructure security and resilience strengthens our ability to share information about how critical infrastructure systems are functioning and the consequence of failures.

These documents reflect input from stakeholders of all viewpoints across Government, industry, and the advocacy community. They include rigorous protections for individual privacy and civil liberties.

Mr. Chairman, the American people expect us to secure the country from the growing threats posed in cyberspace and to ensure that the critical infrastructure of this country is protected. We look forward to working with this committee and with Congress to ensure that we continue to do everything possible to keep the Nation safe and secure.

Thank you very much.

[The prepared statement of Ms. Lute follows:]

PREPARED STATEMENT OF JANE HOLL LUTE

MARCH 13, 2013

Chairman McCaul, Ranking Member Thompson, and Members of the committee: I am pleased to join you today, and I thank the committee for your strong support for the Department of Homeland Security (DHS) over the past 4 years and, indeed, since the Department's founding 10 years ago.

I can think of no more urgent and important topic in today's interconnected world than cybersecurity, and I appreciate the opportunity to explain the Department's mission in this space and how we continue to improve cybersecurity for the American people as well as work to safeguard the Nation's critical infrastructure and protect the Federal Government's networks.

CURRENT THREAT LANDSCAPE

Cyberspace is woven into the fabric of our daily lives. According to recent estimates, this global network of networks encompasses more than 2 billion people with at least 12 billion computers and devices, including global positioning systems, mobile phones, satellites, data routers, ordinary desktop computers, and industrial control computers that run power plants, water systems, and more.

While this increased connectivity has led to significant transformations and advances across our country—and around the world—it also has increased the importance and complexity of our shared risk. Our daily life, economic vitality, and National security depend on cyberspace. A vast array of interdependent IT networks, systems, services, and resources are critical to communication, travel, powering our homes, running our economy, and obtaining Government services. No country, industry, community, or individual is immune to cyber risks. The word "cybersecurity" itself encompasses protection against a broad range of malicious activity, from denial-of-service attacks, to theft of valuable trade secrets, to intrusions against Government networks and systems that control our critical infrastructure.

The United States confronts a dangerous combination of known and unknown vulnerabilities in cyberspace and strong and rapidly expanding adversary capabilities. Cyber crime has also increased significantly over the last decade. Sensitive information is routinely stolen from both Government and private-sector networks, undermining the integrity of the data contained within these systems. We currently see malicious cyber activity from foreign nations engaged in espionage and information warfare, terrorists, organized crime, and insiders. Their methods range from distributed denial-of-service (DDoS) attacks and social engineering to viruses and other malware introduced through thumb drives, supply chain exploitation, and leveraging trusted insiders' access.

We have seen motivations for attacks vary from espionage by foreign intelligence services to criminals seeking financial gain and hackers who may seek bragging rights in the hacker community. Industrial control systems are also targeted by a variety of malicious actors who are usually intent on damaging equipment and facilities or stealing data. Foreign actors are also targeting intellectual property with the goal of stealing trade secrets or other sensitive corporate data from U.S. companies in order to gain an unfair competitive advantage in the global market.

Cyber attacks and intrusions can have very real consequences in the physical world. Last year, DHS identified a campaign of cyber intrusions targeting natural gas and pipeline companies that was highly targeted, tightly focused and well crafted. Stolen information could provide an attacker with sensitive knowledge about industrial control systems, including information that could allow for unauthorized operation of the systems. As the President has said, we know that our adversaries are seeking to sabotage our power grid, our financial institutions, and our air traffic control systems. These intrusions and attacks are coming all the time and they are coming from different sources and take different forms, all the while increasing in seriousness and sophistication.

The U.S. Government has worked closely with the private sector during the recent series of denial-of-service incidents. We have provided classified cyber threat briefings and technical assistance to help banks improve their defensive capabilities and we have increased sharing and coordination among the various Government elements in this area. These developments reinforce the need for Government, industry, and individuals to reduce the ability for malicious actors to establish and maintain capabilities to carry out such efforts.

In addition to these sophisticated attacks and intrusions, we also face a range of traditional crimes that are now perpetrated through cyber networks. These include child pornography and exploitation, as well as banking and financial fraud, all of which pose severe economic and human consequences. For example, in March 2012, the U.S. Secret Service (USSS) worked with U.S. Immigration and Customs Enforcement (ICE) to arrest nearly 20 individuals in its "Operation Open Market," which seeks to combat transnational organized crime, including the buying and selling of stolen personal and financial information through on-line forums. As Americans become more reliant on modern technology, we also become more vulnerable to cyber exploits such as corporate security breaches, social media fraud, and spear phishing, which targets employees through emails that appear to be from colleagues within their own organizations, allowing cyber criminals to steal information.

Cybersecurity is a shared responsibility, and each of us has a role to play. Emerging cyber threats require the engagement of our entire society—from Government and law enforcement to the private sector and, most importantly, members of the public. The key question, then, is how do we address this problem? This is not an easy question because cybersecurity requires a layered approach. The success of our efforts to reduce cybersecurity risks depends on effective identification of cyber threats and vulnerabilities, analysis, and enhanced information sharing between departments and agencies from all levels of government, the private sector, international entities, and the American public.

ROLES, RESPONSIBILITIES, ACTIVITIES

DHS is committed to ensuring cyberspace is supported by a secure and resilient infrastructure that enables open communication, innovation, and prosperity while protecting privacy, confidentiality, and civil rights and civil liberties by design.

Securing Federal Civilian Government Networks

DHS has operational responsibilities for securing unclassified Federal civilian government networks and working with owners and operators of critical infrastructure to secure their networks through cyber threat analysis, risk assessment, mitigation, and incident response capabilities. We also are responsible for coordinating the National response to significant cyber incidents and for creating and maintaining a common operational picture for cyberspace across the Government.

DHS directly supports Federal civilian departments and agencies in developing capabilities that will improve their cybersecurity posture in accordance with the Federal Information Security Management Act (FISMA). To protect Federal civilian agency networks, our National Protection and Programs Directorate (NPPD) is deploying technology to detect and block intrusions through the National Cybersecurity Protection System and its EINSTEIN protective capabilities, while providing guidance on what agencies need to do to protect themselves and measuring implementation of those efforts.

NPPD is also developing a Continuous Monitoring as a Service capability, which will result in an array of sensors that feed data about an agency's cybersecurity risk and present those risks in an automated and continuously-updated dashboard visible to technical workers and managers to enhance agencies' ability to see and counteract day-to-day cyber threats. This capability will support compliance with administration policy, be consistent with guidelines set forth by the National Institute of Standards and Technology (NIST), and enable Federal agencies to move from compliance-driven risk management to data-driven risk management. These activities will provide organizations with information necessary to support risk response decisions, security status information, and on-going insight into effectiveness of security controls.

Protecting Critical Infrastructure

Critical infrastructure is the backbone of our country's National and economic security. It includes power plants, chemical facilities, communications networks, bridges, highways, and stadiums, as well as the Federal buildings where millions of Americans work and visit each day. DHS coordinates the National protection, prevention, mitigation, and recovery from cyber incidents and works regularly with business owners and operators to take steps to strengthen their facilities and communities. The Department also conducts on-site risk assessments of critical infrastructure and shares risk and threat information with State, local, and private-sector partners.

Protecting critical infrastructure against growing and evolving cyber threats requires a layered approach. DHS actively collaborates with public and private sector partners every day to improve the security and resilience of critical infrastructure while responding to and mitigating the impacts of attempted disruptions to the Nation's critical cyber and communications networks and to reduce adverse impacts on critical network systems.

DHS enhances situational awareness among stakeholders, including those at the State and local level, as well as industrial control system owners and operators, by providing critical cyber threat, vulnerability, and mitigation data, including through Information Sharing and Analysis Centers, which are cybersecurity resources for critical infrastructure sectors. DHS is also home to the National Cybersecurity & Communications Integration Center (NCCIC), a 24×7 cyber situational awareness, incident response, and management center that is a National nexus of cyber and communications integration for the Federal Government, intelligence community, and law enforcement.

Responding to Cyber Threats

DHS is responsible for coordinating the Federal Government response to significant cyber or physical incidents affecting critical infrastructure. Since 2009, the NCCIC has responded to nearly half a million incident reports and released more than 26,000 actionable cybersecurity alerts to our public and private-sector partners. The DHS Office of Intelligence and Analysis is a key partner in NCCIC activities, providing tailored all-source cyber threat intelligence and warning to NCCIC components and public and private critical infrastructure stakeholders to prioritize risk analysis and mitigation.

An integral player within the NCCIC, the U.S. Computer Emergency Readiness Team (US–CERT) also provides response support and defense against cyber attacks for Federal civilian agency networks as well as private-sector partners upon request. US–CERT collaborates and shares information with State and local government, industry, and international partners, consistent with rigorous privacy, confidentiality, and civil liberties guidelines, to address cyber threats and develop effective security responses. In 2012, US–CERT processed approximately 190,000 cyber incidents involving Federal agencies, critical infrastructure, and our industry partners. This represents a 68 percent increase from 2011. In addition, US–CERT issued over 7,455 actionable cyber-alerts in 2012 that were used by private-sector and Government agencies to protect their systems, and had over 6,400 partners subscribe to the US–CERT portal to engage in information sharing and receive cyber threat warning information.

The Department's Industrial Control Systems Cyber Emergency Response Team (ICS–CERT) also responded to 177 incidents last year while completing 89 site assistance visits and deploying 15 teams with US–CERT to respond to significant private-sector cyber incidents. DHS also empowers owners and operators through a cyber self-evaluation tool, which was used by over 1,000 companies last year, as well as in-person and on-line training sessions.

Successful response to dynamic cyber threats requires leveraging homeland security, law enforcement, and military authorities and capabilities, which respectively promote domestic preparedness, criminal deterrence and investigation, and National defense. DHS, the Department of Justice (DOJ), and the Department of Defense (DOD) each play a key role in responding to cybersecurity incidents that pose a risk to the United States. In addition to the aforementioned responsibilities of our Department, DOJ is the lead Federal department responsible for the investigation, attribution, disruption, and prosecution of domestic cybersecurity incidents while DOD is responsible for securing National security and military systems as well as gathering foreign cyber threat information and defending the Nation from attacks in cyberspace. DHS supports our partners in many ways. For example, the United States Coast Guard as an Armed Force has partnered with U.S. Cyber Command and U.S. Strategic Command to conduct military cyberspace operations.

While each agency operates within the parameters of its authorities, the U.S. Government's response to cyber incidents of consequence is coordinated among these three agencies such that "a call to one is a call to all." Synchronization among DHS, DOJ, and DOD not only ensures that whole-of-Government capabilities are brought to bear against cyber threats, but also improves Government's ability to share timely and actionable cybersecurity information among a variety of partners, including the private sector.

Combating Cyber Crime

DHS employs more law enforcement agents than any other Department in the Federal Government and has personnel stationed in every State and in more than 75 countries around the world. To combat cyber crime, DHS relies upon the skills and resources of the USSS and ICE and works in cooperation with partner organizations to investigate cyber criminals. Since 2009, DHS has prevented $10 billion in potential losses through cyber crime investigations and arrested more than 5,000 individuals for their participation in cyber crime activities.

The Department leverages the 31 USSS Electronic Crimes Task Forces (ECTF), which combine the resources of academia, the private sector, and local, State, and Federal law enforcement agencies to combat computer-based threats to our financial payment systems and critical infrastructure. A recently executed partnership between ICE Homeland Security Investigations and USSS demonstrates the Department's commitment to leveraging capability and finding efficiencies. Both organizations will expand participation in the existing ECTFs. In addition to strengthening each agency's cyber investigative capabilities, this partnership will produce benefits with respect to the procurement of computer forensic hardware, software licensing, and training that each agency requires. The Department is also a partner in the National Cyber Investigative Joint Task Force, which serves as a collaborative entity that fosters information sharing across the interagency.

We work with a variety of international partners to combat cyber crime. For example, through the U.S.-E.U. Working Group on Cybersecurity and Cybercrime, which was established in 2010, we develop collaborative approaches to a wide range of cybersecurity and cyber crime issues. In 2011, DHS participated in the Cyber Atlantic tabletop exercise, a U.S.-E.U. effort to enhance international collaboration of incident management and response, and in 2012, DHS and the European Union signed a joint statement that advances transatlantic efforts to enhance on-line safety for children. ICE also works with international partners to seize and destroy counterfeit goods and disrupt websites that sell these goods. Since 2010, ICE and its partners have seized over 2,000 domain names associated with businesses selling counterfeit goods over the internet. To further these efforts, the administration issued its Strategy on Mitigating the Theft of U.S. Trade Secrets last month. DHS will act vigorously to support the Strategy's efforts to combat the theft of U.S. trade secrets—especially in cases where trade secrets are targeted through illicit cyber activity by criminal hackers.

In addition, the National Computer Forensic Institute has trained more than 1,000 State and local law enforcement officers since 2009 to conduct network intrusion and electronic crimes investigations and forensic functions. Several hundred prosecutors and judges as well as representatives from the private sector have also received training on the impact of network intrusion incident response, electronic crimes investigations, and computer forensics examinations.

Building Partnerships

DHS serves as the focal point for the Government's cybersecurity outreach and awareness efforts. Raising the cyber education and awareness of the general public creates a more secure environment in which the private or financial information of individuals is better protected. For example, the Multi-State Information Sharing and Analysis Center (MS–ISAC) opened its Cyber Security Operations Center in November 2010, which has enhanced NCCIC situational awareness at the State and local government level and allows the Federal Government to quickly and efficiently provide critical cyber threat, risk, vulnerability, and mitigation data to State and local governments. MS–ISAC has since grown to include all 50 States, three U.S. territories, the District of Columbia, and more than 200 local governments.

The Department also has established close working relationships with industry through partnerships like the Protected Critical Infrastructure Information (PCII) Program, which enhances voluntary information sharing between infrastructure owners and operators and the Government. The Cyber Information Sharing and Collaboration Program established a systematic approach to cyber threat information sharing and collaboration between critical infrastructure owners and operators across the various sectors. And, in 2010, we launched a National campaign called "Stop.Think.Connect" to spread public awareness about how to keep our cyber networks safe.

In addition, DHS works closely with international partners to enhance information sharing, increase situational awareness, improve incident response capabilities, and coordinate strategic policy issues in support of the administration's International Strategy for Cyberspace. For example, the Department has fostered international partnerships in support of capacity building for cybersecurity through agreements with Computer Emergency Response and Readiness Teams as well as the DHS Science & Technology Directorate (S&T). Since 2009, DHS has established partnerships with Australia, Canada, Egypt, India, Israel, the Netherlands, and Sweden.

Fostering Innovation

The Federal Government relies on a variety of stakeholders to pursue effective research and development projects that address increasingly sophisticated cyber threats. This includes research and development activities by the academic and scientific communities to develop capabilities that protect citizens by enhancing the resilience, security, integrity, and accessibility of information systems used by the private sector and other critical infrastructure. DHS supports Centers of Academic Excellence around the country to cultivate a growing number of professionals with expertise in various disciplines, including cybersecurity.

DHS S&T is leading efforts to develop and deploy more secure internet protocols that protect consumers and industry internet users. We continue to support leap-ahead research and development, targeting revolutionary techniques and capabilities that can be deployed over the next decade with the potential to redefine the state of cybersecurity in response to the Comprehensive National Cybersecurity Initiative. For example, DHS was a leader in the development of protocols at the Internet Engineering Task Force called Domain Name System Security (DNS SEC) Extensions. DNS SEC is necessary to protect internet users from being covertly redirected to malicious websites and helps prevent theft, fraud, and abuse on-line by blocking bogus page elements and flagging pages whose Domain Name System (DNS) identity has been hijacked. S&T is also driving improvements through a

Transition to Practice Program as well as liability and risk management protections provided by the Support Anti-Terrorism by Fostering Effective Technology (SAFE-TY) Act that promote cybersecurity technologies and encourage their transition into successful use.

Growing and Strengthening our Cyber Workforce

We know it only takes a single infected computer to potentially infect thousands and perhaps millions of others. But at the end of the day, cybersecurity is ultimately about people. The most impressive and sophisticated technology is worthless if it's not operated and maintained by informed and conscientious users.

To help us achieve our mission, we have created a number of competitive scholarship, fellowship, and internship programs to attract top talent. We are growing our world-class cybersecurity workforce by creating and implementing standards of performance, building and leveraging a cybersecurity talent pipeline with secondary and post-secondary institutions Nation-wide, and institutionalizing an effective, ongoing capability for strategic management of the Department's cybersecurity workforce. Congress can support this effort by pursuing legislation that provides DHS with the hiring and pay flexibilities we need to secure Federal civilian networks, protect critical infrastructure, respond to cyber threats, and combat cyber crime.

RECENT EXECUTIVE ACTIONS

As discussed above, America's National security and economic prosperity are increasingly dependent upon the cybersecurity of critical infrastructure. With today's physical and cyber infrastructure growing more inextricably linked, critical infrastructure and emergency response functions are inseparable from the information technology systems that support them. The Government's role in this effort is to share information and encourage enhanced security and resilience, while identifying and addressing gaps not filled by the marketplace.

Last month, President Obama issued Executive Order 13636 on Improving Critical Infrastructure Cybersecurity as well as Presidential Policy Directive 21 on Critical Infrastructure Security and Resilience, which will strengthen the security and resilience of critical infrastructure through an updated and overarching National framework that acknowledges the increased role of cybersecurity in securing physical assets.

DHS Responsibilities

The President's actions mark an important milestone in the Department's ongoing efforts to coordinate the National response to significant cyber incidents while enhancing the efficiency and effectiveness of our work to strengthen the security and resilience of critical infrastructure. The Executive Order supports more efficient sharing of cyber threat information with the private sector and directs NIST to develop a Cybersecurity Framework to identify and implement better security practices among critical infrastructure sectors. The Executive Order directs DHS to establish a voluntary program to promote the adoption of the Cybersecurity Framework in conjunction with Sector-Specific Agencies and to work with industry to assist companies in implementing the framework.

The Executive Order also expands the voluntary DHS Enhanced Cybersecurity Service program, which promotes cyber threat information sharing between Government and the private sector. This engagement helps critical infrastructure entities protect themselves against cyber threats to the systems upon which so many Americans rely. This program is a good example of information sharing with confidentiality, privacy, and civil liberties protections built into its structure. DHS will share with appropriately-cleared private-sector cybersecurity providers the same threat indicators that we rely on to protect the .gov domain. Those providers will then be free to contract with critical infrastructure entities and provide cybersecurity services comparable to those provided to the U.S. Government.

Through the Executive Order, the President also directed agencies to incorporate privacy, confidentiality, and civil liberties protections. It specifically instructs DHS to issue a public report on activities related to implementation, which would therefore enhance the existing privacy policy, compliance, and oversight programs of DHS and the other agencies.

In addition, the Presidential Policy Directive directs the Executive branch to strengthen our capability to understand and efficiently share information about how well critical infrastructure systems are functioning and the consequences of potential failures. It also calls for a comprehensive research and development plan for critical infrastructure to guide the Government's effort to enhance market-based innovation.

Because the vast majority of U.S. critical infrastructure is owned and operated by private companies, reducing the risk to these vital systems requires a strong partnership between Government and industry. There is also a role for State, local, Tribal, and territorial governments who own a significant portion of the Nation's critical infrastructure. In developing these documents, the administration sought input from stakeholders of all viewpoints in industry, Government, and the advocacy community.

Their input has been vital in crafting an order that incorporates the best ideas and lessons learned from public and private-sector efforts while ensuring that our information sharing incorporates rigorous protections for individual privacy, confidentiality, and civil liberties. Indeed, as we perform all of our cyber-related work, we are mindful of the need to protect privacy, confidentiality, and civil liberties. The Department has implemented strong privacy and civil rights and civil liberties standards into all its cybersecurity programs and initiatives from the outset. To accomplish the integrated implementation of these two directives, DHS has established an Interagency Task Force made up of representatives from across all levels of government.

CONTINUING NEED FOR LEGISLATION

It is important to note that the Executive Order directs Federal agencies to work within current authorities and increase voluntary cooperation with the private sector to provide better protection for computer systems critical to our National and economic security. It does not grant new regulatory authority or establish additional incentives for participation in a voluntary program. We continue to believe that a suite of legislation is necessary to implement the full range of steps needed to build a strong public-private partnership, and we will continue to work with Congress to achieve this.

The administration's legislative priorities for the 113th Congress build upon the President's 2011 Cybersecurity Legislative Proposal and take into account 2 years of public and Congressional discourse about how best to improve the Nation's cybersecurity. Congress should enact legislation to incorporate privacy, confidentiality, and civil liberties safeguards into all aspects of cybersecurity; strengthen our critical infrastructure's cybersecurity by further increasing information sharing and promoting the establishment and adoption of standards for critical infrastructure; give law enforcement additional tools to fight crime in the digital age; and create a National Data Breach Reporting requirement.

CONCLUSION

The American people expect us to secure the country from the growing danger of cyber threats and ensure the Nation's critical infrastructure is protected. The threats to our cybersecurity are real, they are serious, and they are urgent.

I look forward to working with this committee and the Congress to ensure we continue to take every step necessary to protect cyber space, in partnership with government at all levels, the private sector, and the American people, and continue to build greater resiliency into critical cyber networks and systems.

I appreciate this committee's guidance and support as together we work to keep our Nation safe. Thank you, again, for the attention you are giving to this urgent matter.

Securing .gov

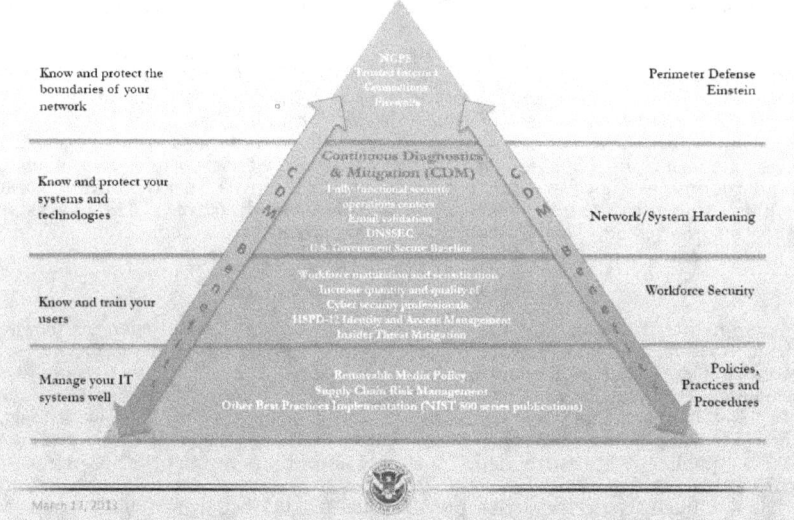

Chairman MCCAUL. I thank the Secretary and I now recognize myself for 5 minutes for questions.

Let me say first, Dr. Lute, how much I enjoyed visiting the NCCIC and our conversation out there and our visit. I would encourage all Members to the extent you haven't been out there to the cyber command center at DHS that you do so.

I think it is a very valuable experience as we move forward towards marking up a bill and getting it on the House floor. I think the Member education process is extremely important in moving forward to protecting the Nation from this very dangerous threat.

You know, we hear every day about attacks from China, the Mandiant report, or military systems, Russia, very sophisticated, Iran—one of the latest ones was particularly disturbing when you hear about a rogue nation like Iran hacking into Aramco's computer systems, 30,000 computers—hard drives erased.

At the same time, a simultaneous attack against our major financial sector. We will hear from the financial sector in the second panel. In fact, JPMorgan was a victim just yesterday.

This is a serious concern. An attack like the one on Aramco and our financial sector could have been extremely chaotic and cause major disruption and destruction.

I wanted to say, in the limited time I have, I am very impressed that, in spite of Congress's failure to act, that you, that the Secretary, that General Alexander with the NSA and Director Mueller with the FBI have come together to actually reach out in a workable arrangement and as I think we look forward to crating legislation, this is a model that I think it provides a good first step in terms of what kind of legislation we are going to mark up on this committee.

I know you referred to threat information almost like a phonebook, you said the Manhattan phonebook, I know you are from New York. But a piece of it in NSA's domain, a piece of it within DHS, you know NSA's more foreign classified threat, DHS threat information, FBI. But what we don't really fail to realize is that majority of this threat information actually resides in the private sector with the critical infrastructures out there.

So I think the goal is how do we create a safe harbor, if you will, where all of these entities can come together and share this threat information in real time, so we can protect not only the interest of the Federal Government but also the critical infrastructures that are out there.

I know you and I talked about the idea of having representatives from the ISAC's, the Information Sharing Analysis Centers, as a full participant on the NCCIC and forward, I think that will be a—certainly a worthwhile goal to pursue.

So with that, let me just turn it over to you in the little bit of time I have and maybe explain this model, how y'all came up with it and how you see the NCCIC moving forward?

Ms. LUTE. Thank you, Mr. Chairman.

I would say the model derived out of Secretary Napolitano's conviction along with Director Mueller and General Alexander, that we needed to pool our strengths in order to share the burden that is being posed to the American public by threats in cybersecurity.

We call there when they meet, we call it the TROIKA and they come together and they speak in very plain terms about how we can operationalize the need to respond to these threats. We can do it by bringing our authorities and our capabilities that, as you see in this chart, are distributed among the three agencies.

You mentioned the analogy of the Manhattan phonebook, and it is true. If you think about the old-fashioned Manhattan phonebook, for those of us who remember it, it was a pretty thick thing.

The government has Q, think of it as that way, and all the rest of the threat information exists out there in the private sector and we need to find ways to share this information in real time. Now that will require better automation, better technology, smarter networks, smarter machines, but also that users, enterprises, and organizations get more savvy as well.

There is a famous saying making the rounds, that there are two kinds of companies in the United States, in the world perhaps, those that have been hacked and those that know they have been hacked.

The status quo is simply unacceptable and the Government is not standing still in the face of that. Our job is to protect society from threats as they emerge. There are threats in cyberspace and we need to mobilize to act. But we need to do it mindful of the role of the private sector. Most of the critical infrastructure is in private-sector hands and we operate on the basis of, or the principle of, nothing about you without you. So sit down with us and let's walk through how we can again, pool all of our strengths to share these burdens.

So of it, as you said, Mr. Chairman will result in greater representation on the NCCIC floor, greater information sharing, greater transparency, but the time to act is now.

Chairman MCCAUL. I certainly agree and I think, you know, we have conducted and I may say, Chairman Pat Meehan of the Cybersecurity Subcommittee has done an outstanding job setting up listening posts, listening to the private sector. We—our philosophy is our bill, we will have buy-in from the stakeholders.

We will have feedback from the private sector about what works and what doesn't work. We believe that our relationship should be a shared relationship with the infrastructures, with the industry rather than a forced one, which I think doesn't work as well, and less proscriptive because it is an ever-evolving area where the law can be quickly behind events.

So, it needs to be agile, it needs to be flexible. The one issue I have heard—now some sectors work very well at DHS like we will hear from the finance sector, of course the oil and gas sector. Others say that they want more participation.

How can you improve, I think DHS and the NCCIC effectiveness, capability, and participation with the private sector, who I believe is really the true partner here?

Ms. LUTE. Thank you, Mr. Chairman.

There are partners that they are true partners, but equally, so are the other partners in the other agencies in the Federal Government, the sector lead agencies that work every day with elements of the critical infrastructure of this country across the 16 sectors of critical infrastructure.

We have prepared and handed out to all of our counterpart agencies and to all of the governors a checklist for understanding the problem posed by cybersecurity. What they should be asking in their organizations, how they should work with their partners in the private sector. We are prepared to bring our expertise together with theirs in these various sectors.

Some sectors are ahead of others, the defense sector for example, IT, telecom, finance as you will hear from. Others are mobilizing and increasingly becoming aware and taking action and we are prepared to support all of those efforts.

Chairman MCCAUL. Yes, the tour I got in the NCCIC, I saw the operations in progress. I know that NSA just did a little sort of pilot program with you where they did share more sensitive information through the civilian portal known as DHS and I think the results were actually quite good and I think the feedback was very positive about the efforts.

I think the civilian interface is important and it is important to a lot of privacy groups I know as well. I know General Alexander actually endorsed that idea that DHS provide that civilian interface to the private sector.

So with the 9 seconds I have, I look forward to working with you, I look forward to working with this committee on drafting important legislation and finally getting this thing done. It has been long overdue. I have been working on this issue for quite some time and I finally feel that the time is right now for the Congress to act for us to get something done and we are working with our Senate counterparts, which is something you didn't see last Congress.

I believe that, you know, Michael Daniel in the White House has been very open and it is something that I think is something that is too important from a National security standpoint to play politics with. It is something we need to get out of this committee, out of the Senate, and signed into law by the President.

So with that, I will now recognize the Ranking Member.

Mr. THOMPSON. Thank you very much, Mr. Chairman.

I look forward to working with you on this committee with respect to our jurisdiction to make sure that we have our opportunity to put the Homeland Security's stamp on whatever goes to the floor.

That being said, Dr. Lute, good seeing you again. We have been missing each other for a while.

President Bush and President Obama both have indicated through various statements and Executive Orders that cybersecurity has to be a priority. With the latest Executive Order from President Obama, can you tell this committee if that Executive Order is satisfactory enough or would you encourage this committee to take on legislation relative to cybersecurity?

Ms. LUTE. Thank you, thanks very much. Good to see you also.

The Executive Order—through the Executive Order, the President has acted within his authorities to direct us to undertake a number of aggressive measures to improve the status quo. We think legislation is still necessary.

We need to enhance information sharing, create incentives for that, incorporate privacy, civil rights, civil liberties, assurances, and safeguards into all aspects of cybersecurity and adopt a framework for cybersecurity standards.

We think Congress has an important role to play, also in affirmatively establishing the positive authority of DHS to protect dot-gov and to help create a National data breach reporting mechanism. So we think there is still a need for legislation and certainly look forward to working with the committee within its jurisdiction to successfully reach that goal.

Mr. THOMPSON. Thank you very much, I am glad you made that point.

The Chairman put a slide on the screen here that talked about a three-part relationship between the DOD, DOJ, and DHS. To some degree, the process is beginning to work, but from what I understand, your testimony today is the roles could be further defined legislatively so that those three agencies can do their work in a better manner. Is that correct?

Ms. LUTE. What I am saying, Mr. Thompson, is that, yes, we think we can—it would be helpful to have legislation clarify and strengthen the role of DHS in protecting .gov, strengthening the tools available to law enforcement, and clarifying that this is a problem of great urgency that the Government is seized with.

Mr. THOMPSON. We received briefings quite a bit on vulnerabilities that exist within cyber. But most of those briefings go in the direction of hackers from China, hackers from Russia, and that is a very significant part of the challenge. But from your testimony, there is also other areas that we should be looking at beyond that.

So most of our briefings for the most part come from a defense posture and I am convinced that that is necessary. But from DHS's perspective, how do you see DHS's role and in managing that cyber jurisdiction that you have?

Ms. LUTE. Well you are talking to an old soldier.

Mr. THOMPSON. Absolutely.

Ms. LUTE. So I certainly understand the role of the Defense Department, and in particular, knowing the National Security Agency as I have since 1978, I understand and value its contribution to the National defense. It absolutely has a role to play.

But cyberspace is civilian space. We need to manage it as civilian space. The status quo is not acceptable. People are under attacks. The attacks that are emanating from actors in China or Iran or Russia or elsewhere around the world are certainly worrisome. We have raised these issues in our diplomatic and other dialogues with appropriate authorities.

But we also know is one of the greatest dangers that we face are the existing vulnerabilities that go unpatched in our systems every single day. They number in the millions. So we have got to take action collectively. Our role, in Homeland Security, and we called this out 4 years ago. We said, essential to helping create a safe, secure, resilient place where the American way of life can thrive, is ensuring our National cybersecurity. We intend to fulfill that responsibility.

Mr. THOMPSON. Thank you very much. Yield back, Mr. Chairman.

Chairman MCCAUL. I thank you Ranking Member. Chairman now recognizes the gentleman from New York, Mr. Peter King.

Mr. KING. Thank you Mr. Chairman. Secretary Lute, great to see you back here. Thank you very much. Let me commend the Chairman for going forth with this hearing. This is absolutely essential that legislation be passed. I believe that DHS and this committee have a vital role to play in that, in those regards. Without setting up a competition but showing seamless cooperation. What unique capacity does DHS bring to the table, let's say separate from the FBI, separate from DOD? Why is it essential that DHS be part of the final answer?

Ms. LUTE. Thank you, good to see you also. When you think about the expertise and the resources and the authorities and jurisdictions that each of the departments bring, DOD is responsible, General Alexander, responsible for securing dot-mil. Dot-mil, if I can be allowed a comparison, is the size of this pen cap. Dot-gov is the size of this box in front of me. Dot-com is the size of this room. And growing. Organically and instantaneously every single day.

What we bring is our working relationship with the private sector. The responsibility to coordinate National protection efforts on behalf of the Federal Government. The responsibility to secure dot-gov. Now I have handed out, and I hope you have all received our strategy for securing dot-gov. That addresses issues, and we have policies and capabilities and staff, that assist the Federal agencies in managing their IT systems well. Knowing and training the users, the administrators of their systems, knowing, understanding and protecting the systems and technologies and the boundaries of the network as well.

Our job, and we take it seriously, is to prevent bad things from happening and respond rapidly when we do. We have extraordinary men and women who work in the Department on this. In fact, our

ICS–CERT, our Industrial Control Systems Cybersecurity Emergency Response Team, was just highlighted by SC magazine as the No. 1 cybersecurity team in the country. We take great pride in that.

So we bring this perspective and this additional set of responsibilities and authorities and capabilities to bear.

Mr. KING. At the current moment, do you believe that DHS has sufficient resources to implement and carry out the Executive Order?

Ms. LUTE. We are, we are undertaking to carry out the Executive Order and devising on an aggressive time table, the plans, the approaches, the frameworks, and the inputs. Those resourcing decisions will need to be made in the context when that work is completed. But we have mobilized ourselves internally, created a task organization within the Department, across every aspect of the Department, to get that work done in response to the President's direction.

Mr. KING. On the issue of the hostile power cyber breaches, to the extent you can discuss it in open forum, if you could refer to the Mandiant report and the impact of China hacking into the United States. The significance of that, and could you just drive home how significant that is?

Ms. LUTE. Well we believe it is extraordinarily significant and what I would say about the Mandiant report only, is that it is illustrative of the extraordinary capability that exists in the American private sector in the area of cybersecurity. We really have some of the best in the world in this country. When it comes to technology, expertise, insight, analysis, and perseverance, with what is a growing problem.

Second, what I would say is, I guess I would echo what Tom Donilon said recently in a speech on the question of China, we have raised this issue of the attacks that are emanating from actors in China, with Chinese authorities. We have called on them to acknowledge it, take it seriously, understand it. To investigate it and stop it and to work with us in creating broad norms of responsible cyber behavior.

Mr. KING. Would you say that Mandiant is typical or atypical of cooperation between Government and the private sector?

Ms. LUTE. What I would say is that it is the leading edge of what will be best practice.

Mr. KING. Okay. Do you intend to pursue that type of relationship?

Ms. LUTE. Absolutely.

Mr. KING. Yes, okay.

Ms. LUTE. What is very clear, Chairman, is that no single entity can do all that needs doing here. Partnering with the private sector is an intrinsic part of our approach to cybersecurity.

Mr. KING. Secretary, thank you very much. Yield back. Thank you.

Chairman MCCAUL. The gentleman, the Chairman now recognizes the gentlelady from California, Ms. Sanchez.

Ms. SANCHEZ. Thank you Mr. Chairman and thank you Secretary for being before us. This is an issue that many of us have been working on this for a while. I have the opportunity to sit on the Armed Services Committee and do cybersecurity from that end.

There are many people, let me begin by saying, I congratulate you in working across so many agencies and departments with respect to this in the Executive arena. I know that in the House and the Senate, those of us who work on this on different committees sometimes don't even know we are all working on it. So I congratulate you on that.

But there are some of my colleagues who feel that the total answer to this is our Defense Department. I find that, especially when I am sitting with Intel members or with HASC members or people who are very comfortable, if you will, with the military. So sitting also on this committee, I understand there is just so much more to be done than just to use our Department of Defense or some of those agencies and initiatives on the rest of this.

Can you, can you do me a favor and walk through currently what, how you are involved and what the situation would look like for example? Let's say a big telecom, maybe AT&T gets hacked and it is ruinous to many people who use, for whatever reason, that company on a daily basis. From the moment we know that something is going wrong, so we have got a private-sector person, company, entity. Then it is important to all of us, because we may do banking through that, or talking to each other, networks. So I would assume you are involved with that. Then who ultimately, you know, who really shuts things down or figures out what went on? Or re-routes what is going on?

Can you sort of walk us through that so that we have an understanding of what the different roles are, private, DHS, military if it is there, et cetera, et cetera?

Ms. LUTE. So thanks very much for that. There is no question that what is going on in cyberspace and on the internet right now, it is contested space. As we all have said, and as we all know, there is a variety of sources of threats and attacks. There is a variety of pre-existing threats and attacks.

Among our most capable industries is the telecom industry. You cited AT&T, certainly they are a leading player in that industry. But the moment of attack is not the point at which to begin our dialogue. We haven't. We are in constant dialogue with AT&T, the other internet providers, other service providers across the critical infrastructures in cyberspace already. We have been doing that now for years.

Together with our partners in DOJ and DOD, who also have their relationships and dialogues with them. So if there is an attack, what we look to see is how well the entity under attack can defend itself. Can we augment that with additional information? Here is where part of what we have been innovating over the past few years is really coming into play.

The government, as I mentioned, has threat information. Can we put that in the hands of the private sector so that they can take appropriate steps to defend themselves? We have proven that we can. This country can protect itself and we will use all of our resources to do so. But we also know that there is a vast amount of information in the private sector.

Can we mobilize that? As kind of a cyber neighborhood watch, so that everyone has the benefit of where the threats might be coming from and when. So we have developed what we call, is a sufficiency framework for defense of the networks, where we step through, beginning at the entity level, the agency or the organization's level. Are they doing everything they can? Can they be augmented by us? By the FBI? By other parts of the Federal Government or other parts of government usefully? Can we step through that to ensure that we prevent bad things from happening and that we respond and mitigate immediately when they do?

Ms. SANCHEZ. At what point, because we have read, in places, that more and more are experts within Intel and Defense are aiding, if you will, some of these private entities. At what point would they swoop in to save the situation?

Ms. LUTE. So we work side-by-side with our partners in the Federal Government, including in the intelligence agency, appropriately under rules. Also mindful of the responsibilities to, that we all have within our authorities. We will not manage the cybersecurity of this Nation as an Intel program. No one is suggesting that.

What we do want to do is mobilize all of the resources that we have in the Federal Government to address the status quo which is unacceptable.

Ms. SANCHEZ. Thank you, Secretary. I have other questions, but I will submit them for the record. Thank you for your work in this.

Ms. LUTE. Thank you.

Chairman McCAUL. Chairman now recognizes the Committee—Cybersecurity Subcommittee Chairman, Mr. Meehan, out of order, and ask for unanimous consent that he be recognized. Without objection.

Mr. MEEHAN. Thank you, Mr. Chairman.

I am very grateful for the opportunity to join with you on this. I thank you for your leadership in taking this issue at the outset for our committee, because of its importance which I think is being driven home. Not just by our awareness of the events that are taking place within the Nation currently, but the recognition as well as the communications we have had with you and your colleagues across the spectrum, both in the governmental sector and the private sector of the importance of this issue.

While I believe that you have been consistent in the clarion call of recognition on this issue, I think we as a Nation are lagging in an appreciation for the genuine scope of the threat that we face. In addition that the changing nature in that it isn't enough just to be reliant on Government alone, that there is a partnership that is going to be necessary.

I am struck by the reality, 90 percent of the network that we are being tasked with protecting is in the private sector. You clarified that well, so we can, among ourselves in the Government and the Defense Department, NSA, communicate. So I am really interested in how we create this collaboration with the private sector tying back to our Governmental entities. Recognizing of course, as well, that as we get into communication, not just from the Government, what we know to the private sector, but requests from the private sector to share information with the Government that we begin to open the door to other kinds of issues about who gets it, when, where, and what do we do?

Can you just give me an oversight of where the critical parts are in that relationship and how we encourage the private sector to be really engaged in this?

Ms. LUTE. Thank you. In every way, at every level we are working with the private sector. From the meetings that the Secretary has, and the dialogues that I have at my level throughout our organization in Homeland Security, as well again, if I may say in the Department of Justice and in the Department of Defense we meet regularly with the private sector to understand the world in cyberspace from their point of view. But we are also mindful of our role as Government. So we work with the other Federal agencies to—and we have been working to begin to craft a framework, and an approach that will address the unacceptable status quo with respect to cybersecurity attacks.

Every 90 seconds from an operational perspective, US–CERT gets a call about an intrusion. We push out tons of information every day, every week. Recently with the attacks on the financial sector, we have been working with the bureau to put out joint information bulletins, pushing out hundreds of thousands of signatures and information that the private sector can use. We hear uniformly that this has been important and helpful information, and they want more. So this is an evolving partnership, but one that begins from a very solid foundation of respect, mutual regard, and an understanding that no single entity can do all that needs doing.

Mr. MEEHAN. How about the private sector sharing with you though, and not just in a voluntary capacity because you have been great, we have discussed—I had the opportunity with the Chairman among others to spend time talking to some of these entities in New York and otherwise, that are on the front lines of these attacks that are coming across. It is a very sobering situation to see the scope of it. But the—you know those are groups that are coming to you to work together. An issue that we are going to have to struggle with is the whole concept of disclosure by private entities when they know that they have been hacked.

I think you said it well, those that have been hacked, and those that know they have been hacked. That they know they have been hacked, there is an incentive for them to disclose, incentive for them to participate with us. How do we make them partners? Then how do we deal with those who do not wish to disclose and could be in possession of information which is material and important to the defense of our Nation?

Ms. LUTE. Thank you. I won't speak for the private sector, I was raised to speak for myself, and I know you certainly will understand this. But we have heard this, the notion, and we think we understand it, that it does create a burden on this question of disclosure. But there is a far superior burden to the consumers and to the users of this critical infrastructure, if these entities are hacked.

If people's private information has been unlawfully and illegitimately exfiltrated and there is potential for exploitation by cyber criminals or others, in cyber—and we think that we have to address that concern as well. So we look forward to working with

Congress as it contemplates legislation in trying to square this circle.

Mr. MEEHAN. Well my time has expired, but I thank you Mr. Chairman and I also look forward to—I thank you for your observation of the need for legislation that helps clarify a number of things, among which is the framework to allow us to work with you and your—you know your fellow agencies, in an effective way to create this public/private partnership. It is a big task ahead.

Thank you.

Chairman MCCAUL. Let me commend subcommittee Chairman Meehan for his great work in this area, listening to the private sector, and the stakeholders which is vitally important, along with Ms. Clarke from New York, who is now recognized.

Oh, I am sorry, Ms. Jackson Lee is now recognized. Please forgive me.

Ms. JACKSON LEE. Let me thank you very much for your work, Secretary Lute, and I do want to thank my Chairman and Ranking Member, their timing is impeccable. Over the last 24 hours we have heard the proclamations, or proclaiming of a cyber war, cyber threats of major proportion in the next 2 years. So I would like to just hold up to say this is a very informative document, and a very helpful document. As I ask you a series of questions, I do want to make a particular plea.

In the course of answering my question if you might respond to that plea. The plea is that alongside of those who intend to do enormous devastating harm, are those that we call, hackers. Over the last 24 hours, we have heard some of the most provocative hacking in public officials from the First Lady to the former Secretary of State, to a number of entertainers, and I believe that one of our pathways to success is whether or not we can convince these individuals, whether they are benign, whether they happen to be in the category of cerebral persons who want to be stimulated, that they need to work with us, or that this is a dangerous proposition when it comes to the security of the Nation.

Because potentially if we have a cyber war, then are we going to have all of those intervening factors cloud what we are supposed to do to fight those who are truly engaged in terrorism? So I want you to be able to answer that premise of what kind of outreach or understanding do we have of the hacker community? Obviously some are in the category of criminal activities. But if we just sit here in this committee and speak about trying to get our hands around cyber threats, and for example by being aggressive and saying, this is devastating, wind up having all of our systems hacked because we have not communicated how devastating this is, or there is not an outreach or there is not an understanding.

Where are these people at? We are not reaching—finding them either through the investigatory process or not. So I ask that question and I will pause for a moment for you to answer.

Ms. LUTE. Thank you. I don't use the term, war zone or—when I talk about cyberspace. We can't manage the Nation's cybersecurity as if it were a war zone. I mean we have to address this mobilizing all of the resources we have, including the bright and extraordinary young talent that some say make up the hacker world. We have a member of the Homeland Security Advisory Committee,

Jeff Moss who is the founder of DEFCON, and Black Hat, one of the leading organizations that draws on that kind of talent. We have also recently, at the Secretary's instruction, implemented the findings of a cybersecurity workforce, a cyber skills workforce initiative.

This task force, which was chaired by industry leaders in the United States took 90 days and came back to us with ways to raise the skills of our workforce. Ms. Renee Forney sitting behind me, chairs this effort now in the Department. We are going to do five things, and I think these five things are going to in part, appeal to this audience. We are going to hire, test, and train to the very best standards of cybersecurity expertise that exists. We are going to open pipelines, widen the pipelines bringing people, talented young people into Federal service.

We would like them to come to the Department of Homeland Security first, but we will accept their contribution to Government across the board, wherever they go. We are going to work with industry and with academia to do it. We are going to strategically manage our workforce to prize this very valuable talent. This is the place where we really invest in our people. So, this is the way we are going to reach out.

Ms. JACKSON LEE. Let me get these last three questions in. Do you think that the lead role of the DHS is effective now? Bush first established it, now you are in the Obama administration. Two, do you have the flexibility of hiring—you just mentioned it, but do you need more flexibility in hiring the right kind of people? Are you improving the sharing of information between State and local entities from the Federal Government?

Ms. LUTE. Yes, we are up to the task. We need permanent flexibility in our hiring. We can—we will always improve, and can always improve our information sharing, and we are working on that.

Ms. JACKSON LEE. Do you think there will be a cyber war in the next 2 years?

Ms. LUTE. Uh.

Ms. JACKSON LEE. Even though you don't use the word, war?

Ms. LUTE. I was a soldier for a long time——

Ms. JACKSON LEE. I didn't hear you, I am sorry?

Ms. LUTE. I was a soldier for a long time. I think we—cyberspace will remain contentious for some time to come. But there is a lot we can do about it, and are.

Ms. JACKSON LEE. Do you think it can threaten the lifestyle of Americans over the next 2 to 5 years?

Ms. LUTE. Not if I can help it.

Ms. JACKSON LEE. We thank you for your commitment, but I hope that we will have this continuing dialogue. I frankly believe if we do not reach the hacker community, and separate them out from us, trying to fight what can be Government undermining, I think we will have a serious problem. I look forward to working with you. Thank you.

Chairman MCCAUL. I thank the gentlelady from Texas.

The gentleman from Utah, Mr. Stewart, is recognized.

Mr. STEWART. Thank you. I think you have been an excellent witness, you are concise, you illustrate in ways that help us understand, and I appreciate that. I was an Air Force pilot for 14 years. I flew a fairly sophisticated weapons system, but our ROE was fairly straightforward. I mean if we were attacked, we responded. If our forward operating bases were attacked, our infrastructure was attacked, we would respond, and I just don't get the same sense here that there—you know the rules of how we operate are as clear as it was in those examples.

We talk a lot about defend, defend, defend and I would like to spend a few minutes elaborating on your comments on deterrents. My questions I guess would be this: Does the Obama administration view—do they have clear red lines that China or Iran or any other organization knows that they cannot cross? Do they—have we been able to communicate effectively to them what those red lines are? Are we aggressive enough, do you think that that would help to deter future attacks by making them pay the price?

It seems like they ping us all the time with impunity in some cases. That concerns me a little bit, and I would appreciate your response to that concern?

Ms. LUTE. One of the things we know about former—being former military—is that society has entrusted its Government with the responsibility to run the military, keep the Nation safe, defend us from attack. We do that in a physical world. We are better at that than anybody else in the world as well.

What we also know is that not every problem presents itself for a military solution. But there are—nevertheless there is learning, there is information, there is capability, and there is technology that we can derive from our partners in DOD and from our understanding around the world to better defend ourselves against these attacks.

But, as we know, 90 percent of the critical infrastructure in this country is in private-sector hands. We have to involve them in that approach. General Alexander takes the back seat to no one in his willingness, ability, and determination to defend this country, should we reach that point.

I take a back seat to no one, in my commitment to use our civilian resources appropriately under the law to do that as well.

Mr. STEWART. Well, I appreciate your response, but maybe let me press just a little bit on this. That is, again, I don't—help me understand what price these organizations fear or what they feel they are going to pay with some of their—with their constant attacks.

I mean, do they feel like we respond to those and they have anything to lose? Or do they feel like they can operate in this—again, with impunity, without us really pressing them back on that?

Ms. LUTE. There is a—at the moment in cyberspace, offense wins. We know that. I won't speak for how these organizations that are lobbing threats, unlawfully stealing trade secrets and other kinds of crime, quite frankly, in cyberspace, what they think or what motivates them.

What I will say is that we are increasingly making the country aware of the threats posed in cybersecurity. This is present in our dialogues. I have standing conversations with a number of international partners at the homeland security level.

We rely on our diplomats to communicate our diplomatic messages, but at an operator's level we are communicating very clearly as well, behavior that is unacceptable, and trying to find ways that we can—that like-minded governments can work together to stop these actors from acting.

Mr. STEWART. Yes. Well, you know, I appreciate your comment, I really do. Maybe I am not communicating my concern adequately. But again, it just seems to me that we have not instilled a—again, we talk about defend, defend, defend and in your response you mentioned that again and again. But I am not sure that we are aggressive enough in deter and making them pay a price. Am I wrong on that concern, do you think?

Ms. LUTE. I think we are getting better at that all the time. It is an imperative for us. This simply can't go on unimpugned.

Mr. STEWART. Okay. All right.

Mr. Chairman, I yield back.

Chairman MCCAUL. Okay.

The Chairman now recognizes the gentleman from Arizona, Mr. Barber.

Mr. BARBER. Thank you, Mr. Chairman.

The first meeting I came to under your leadership of this committee, I was very pleased to hear that you made cybersecurity a top priority for our committee and for the Congress. I 100 percent agree that that has got to be the case.

My concern is generally, and perhaps you can comment on this, Ms. Lute, is the public, it seems to me, is pretty much unaware of the threat that this poses to the homeland, to the country. I think traditionally, you know, we think of protecting the homeland, protecting our Nation, as military protection or police protection. This issue is not a very visible issue at all, unfortunately, for most people.

Could you comment on what we can and should be doing, both in the administration and in Congress and in the public at large to make people more aware of the imminent danger of cyber attacks and how we can get public support for taking the necessary action?

Ms. LUTE. Thank you very much for this question. Part of the problem is strategic, centralized, and top-driven, the threats that we perceive in cyberspace to National security. We are addressing them.

But cyberspace is transactional, decentralized, and bottom-driven. So is homeland security. We are transaction-based, decentralized, bottom-driven. In our world, it is not so much need-to-know, it is duty-to-share, when we are talking about information.

So we are working aggressively to put the word out. A lot of people are unaware. We have been promoting, through a cyber education program, such things as "Stop. Think. Connect," so that people engage intellectually before they get on-line, so they understand cyber threats. We have more to do in this regard, but equally, citizens, companies, State and local government, every aspect of our society needs to get engaged.

Mr. BARBER. Thank you for that. I just want to add to the gentleman's earlier comment that we see a lot of witnesses in Congress and I really want to commend you on your clarity and your brevity in responding to our questions and in your initial opening statement.

I have a question related to the recent Inspector General's audit of the Industrial Control Systems Cyber Emergency Response Team. It found that although the team has made significant progress in building out its capabilities to support critical infrastructure owners and operators, the challenges still remain, particularly in the sharing of timely and actionable threat information.

Could you please comment on the challenge of balancing the need to get information to critical infrastructure in time to stop attacks, while protecting intelligent sources and methods?

Ms. LUTE. We are working on that.

Sorry, I beg your pardon.

I would be happy to talk in greater detail in a different setting. It is not—it is a significant issue. How do we share information appropriately? But not only between the Government and the private sector, but between the private-sector entities themselves. I see US–CERT as the best in the country.

Mr. BARBER. Very good. I certainly want to commend the Secretary for the action that she has taken and the priority she has given and, through you, carrying out this action within DHS.

I am firmly of the belief that we have to have legislation. We have to have legislation that improves and increases our capabilities to stop these attacks, both on the private as well as the public web sites and infrastructure. I also believe that we have to figure out a way to make sure we have—assure people that we are protecting their privacy.

So to the question about hackers. As we work to improve cybersecurity, I want to know more about what we can do to penalize those who perpetrate cyber attacks. That we send—how do we send a clear message to our cyber adversaries of the high cost of attacking the United States?

Also, could you talk about what we can do to hold hackers who are not friendly, in any way, accountable for their actions?

Ms. LUTE. Thank you for that. Two aspects to my answer. No. 1, we need to strengthen the hand of law enforcement to enforce the law. To a large extent, what we are seeing in cyberspace is crime. We need to give our law enforcement officers the tools they need to investigate, pursue, and successfully prosecute the crimes that occur in cyberspace. We are working very closely, Secret Service, Immigration Customs Enforcement, working very closely with the FBI, other law enforcement agencies, to do just that. We are getting better all the time. Here is an area where legislation can help.

A word, if I may, on privacy, civil rights and civil liberties. We can do both. We can ensure your cybersecurity while protecting your civil rights and civil liberties. It must remain a dual imperative.

Mr. BARBER. Thank you, Mr. Chairman. You can count on my support for legislation. This has to be a bipartisan issue and I appreciate your leadership and that of the Ranking Member.

Chairman MCCAUL. I thank the gentleman. I agree with you on the capability issue, as well. Also, Dr. Lute, on the balance of privacy versus security. It is hugely important and I think DHS is well-suited for that.

The Chairman now recognizes the gentleman from Pennsylvania, Mr. Rothfus.

Mr. ROTHFUS. Thank you, Mr. Chairman.

Thank you, Madam Secretary, for being here today. This is very informative for me.

I understand the collaboration that exists now between DHS, the Defense Department, and the Department of Justice, FBI. A question that occurs to me is whether or not we currently have any Federal official who is the primary point of contact for the oversight of cybersecurity?

Ms. LUTE. So we would say that the Secretary of Homeland Security is responsible for coordinating across the Government, but we work collaboratively with our partners in DOJ and DOD.

Mr. ROTHFUS. So the Secretary would convene meetings of these other agencies to ensure that collaboration is taking place as appropriate——

Ms. LUTE. Also attend. The responsibility for securing dot-mil belongs with DOD and in other sectors, and of course, the lead law enforcement investigative agency is the FBI.

Mr. ROTHFUS. If I could just——

Ms. LUTE. I beg your pardon.

Mr. ROTHFUS. Thank you. A couple of questions as I review the organizational structure of the Department of Homeland Security and whether or not you are as organized as optimal.

We appear to have a number of offices within the Department that address cybersecurity. Under Science and Technology, we have the Office of Cybersecurity Division, where we have US–CERT, as I understand it. Under National Protection and Programs Directorate, we have the Office of Cybersecurity and Communications. Then under Intelligence and Analysis we have another Office of Cyber, Infrastructure, and Science.

None of these offices that appear to deal with cybersecurity directly report to the Secretary. If you could just share with us how that works, how that information is channeled to the Secretary from these disparate offices, and whether or not there should be consideration for any kind of reorganization within the Department, given the importance of cybersecurity?

Ms. LUTE. The Secretary maintains constant awareness of where we are in cybersecurity and is very up to speed on every aspect of the operations of the offices that you described.

As chief operating officer of the Department, my job is to see that everything is running. Every Wednesday, I chair a 3-hour cybersecurity meeting among all of those agencies.

This is like so much else. I am an operator. Operations conform to functions and needs that agencies or, in our case, the Federal Government require. Is our organizational structure optimal? I don't know of any such thing sort of anywhere. It is a constantly-evolving process.

The issue of direct report may, at a surface level, communicate salience, importance, or ease of access. The Secretary places extreme importance on the cyber activities of the Department, has no problem getting access or answers to any question or issue that may arise, and we maintain constant vigilance over all of these parts of the Department.

So can we change and improve? Of course. What will drive us? We have got a cybersecurity strategy. We have laid out an approach to securing dot-gov, we are engaging the private sector and the American people on an educational platform, as well, as I mentioned.

We will adapt our organization to these imperatives as we move along. We are paying a lot of attention to this.

Mr. ROTHFUS. Thank you.

We have some great assets in southwestern Pennsylvania with University of Pittsburgh, Carnegie Mellon University. I am just curious how you are leveraging, if at all, the capacities of our academic institutions in this effort.

Ms. LUTE. Well-known to us, great partners in the analytics side, I mean our S&T, you mentioned Science and Technology, Doug Maughan who heads our cybersecurity work on that front. It is a National treasure. He knows these organizations, is well-known to them. So we leverage them a lot as we can.

I mentioned also in response to an early question, our desire to broaden the pipeline of talent that comes into homeland security, working with academia and with industry as well.

Mr. ROTHFUS. Thank you.

I yield back.

Chairman MCCAUL. Thank you to the gentleman.

The Chairman now recognizes the gentleman from New Jersey, Mr. Payne.

Mr. PAYNE. Thank you, Mr. Chairman.

It is very good to see you once again.

You know, we have been talking a lot about the different Government departments are working well together, sharing information in terms of this whole issue. But it seems like it is still a challenge and I hear you saying that the private sector is coming along. But you know, much progress has been made with NCCIC program. You said that we need to get private entities on board.

Specifically, what legislation can be passed to create incentives for that?

Ms. LUTE. Thank you, Congressman Payne and Mr. Chairman with your permission, I would just like to acknowledge Congressman Payne's father's passing a year ago last week. He was one of my father's closest friends. He admired him and appreciated the work he did. I may be a New Yorker, I was born in Newark, and I have never forgotten it, and I just would like to acknowledge with respect and appreciation his work, Congressman and yours as well on behalf of the people from someplace I call home.

Chairman MCCAUL. We all share in that our condolences to you and your father.

Mr. PAYNE. Yes, and to you ma'am, your father played a great part in recognizing my father's commitment to public service very early on when a lot of people doubted it and he was one of the people that really helped open the door for him and we see what he was able to accomplish. So to your family, I thank you as well.

So, in terms of the legislation to create incentive?

Ms. LUTE. So, many of the ideas in the cyber EO, draw on the House Republicans Cyber Taskforce. We think additional legislation in terms of enhancing information sharing and creating incentives for industry to participate with us and adopting standards and best practices.

For example, we know today, we know today, that we can—we have the technology to identify hardware that is on systems, white list software that is acceptable to be on systems, understand network configurations and have machines talk to each other in real time to identify threat factors and respond and patch in real time.

We think that by sharing this information and creating a culture of accountability and action that industry will be incentivized to act. We need Congress's help in this regard and we look forward to working with the committee to achieve that.

Mr. PAYNE. Okay.

But it—I know there has been some difficulty in getting these private entities to buy in at times and even admit that they have been hacked and have had problems. It is almost like having a bully and you are scared to say that you have been attacked by this bully because it shows some type of weakness. How do we get them to even admit that they have had issues when a lot of them hold back that information?

Ms. LUTE. We think an important component of legislation would be establishing a National data breach reporting system and we have changed the culture, not completely, in the example that you cite. We need to change the culture here because as problematic as it—as some may think it might be to report on a breach, it is far more problematic when the breach goes unreported and far more problematic when people's privacy and their private information goes exfiltrated unlawfully. We need to address that and close that gap.

Mr. PAYNE. Thank you.

I think I will yield back, Mr. Chairman.

Chairman MCCAUL. The gentleman—and I—let me just point out, I think the liability protections that we will be looking at can greatly incentivize the private sector to share the information and provide that safe harbor that they can go to which we envision to be the, you know, the NCCIC itself. So, let me also on a point of personal privilege, your father and I worked on the Sudan caucus and I know he founded that caucus and was just a great soul and we miss him.

Mr. PAYNE. Thank you.

Chairman MCCAUL. With that, I now recognize the gentleman from Mississippi, Mr. Palazzo.

Mr. PALAZZO. Thank you, Mr. Chairman and I would like to thank Ms. Lute for being here today. Thank you for your testimony and also thank you for the vital service that you provide and protecting our homeland from threats and your dedication and your military service is also commendable as one soldier to another. I was a former Marine, now a soldier to a soldier, okay. I had to put that in there, I might get in trouble. I have a gunnery sergeant in my office serving as the military fellow. But anyway, I digress.

Listen, protecting our private and our public sector from cyber attacks is extremely important. But in the interest of time, I would also like to know, you know, what does Department of Homeland Security do to protect their own information? Because I am aware the Department uses the National Center for Critical Information

Processing and Storage which is also known as NCCIPS, to house Nationally-sensitive critical or classified information, hundreds of millions of dollars have been invested in massive and redundant infrastructure and IT equipment to ensure uninterrupted service to multiple Federal agencies who share this facility.

So given the amount of sensitive information the Department stores at the center, how secure is the center as well as DHS assets from potential cyber attacks?

Ms. LUTE. Thank you for that.

We are the largest tenant. I think three-quarters of the data center is leased by us for secure data processing and storage. We adopt as we do in other aspects of homeland security, a layered approach, from perimeter fences, roving patrols, armed access gates, guards, CCTV, facility control systems, fully redundant power supplies.

What we are trying to model in homeland security is best practice across the range of activities that we have said is necessary to secure dot-gov, from being aware on how to well manage our IT systems, understand who has access, et cetera. But it is a layered approach involving physical as well as cyber measures.

Mr. PALAZZO. As we focus on how we protect our information and prevent cyber attacks, should the Department and other Federal agencies use NCCIPS as a model for securing sensitive information?

Ms. LUTE. We think it represents an approach to best practice who, again, incorporates not only physical but cybersecurities as well.

Mr. PALAZZO. So it is a good model?

Ms. LUTE. It is a good model.

Mr. PALAZZO. For other agencies to adopt?

Ms. LUTE. Yes.

Mr. PALAZZO. It is secure?

Ms. LUTE. Yes.

Mr. PALAZZO. Safe?

Ms. LUTE. Yes.

Mr. PALAZZO. All right, now——

Ms. LUTE. Mississippi, I spent a year in Mississippi, so——

Mr. PALAZZO. Not in August, right?

Ms. LUTE. In August, it was hot.

Mr. PALAZZO. Bless your heart.

It—real quick, to just change a little bit and I don't think anybody has really touched—I know China has come up a couple of times. You know, my experience with the Chinese hasn't, you know, really been pleasant from the sense that, you know, after Katrina, they flooded our markets with contaminated drywall, you know, constantly hearing about their products being dangerous to children, you know, coated in lead-based paint and so on.

Then you look at—from a military standpoint, they are building up their military and to hear the report that came out 2 weeks ago that there is blatant attacks by the Chinese government that is kind of attacking our systems. Can you elaborate just real quickly on the cyber threat posed by China and any plans this administration has in deterring China from continuing to steal U.S. intellectual property and other assets from the public and private sectors?

What would be our red line that we say they cannot cross before we retaliate?

Ms. LUTE. Congressman, what I will say in this forum, and I am happy to pursue this in an appropriate forum other than here, is that we are concerned about the attacks that seem—appear to be emanating from actors within China. We made this very clear. We have called on Chinese authorizes to recognize and address this, to investigate it, pursue it, and to work with us in establishing collaborative norms. We take this very seriously.

Mr. PALAZZO. Thank you.

I yield back.

Chairman MCCAUL. The Chairman now recognizes the—let's see here, hold on second, the—yes, the gentleman from Texas, Mr. O'Rourke.

Mr. O'ROURKE. Thank you. Thank you, Mr. Chairman.

Secretary Lute, thank you for your testimony today and the quality of your answers to the questions asked so far.

A lot of analogies have been made today to physical space and cyberspace, physical security and cybersecurity and one that I would like you to respond to is the analogy between border security and cybersecurity and one of the challenges we have had as a committee and a Congress is defining what border security is and we are spending $18 billion on it today, twice what we were spending in 2006. We have doubled the size of the Border Patrol. A lot of important future legislation hinges on our answer to it, and we are unable to define it.

I can see perhaps as cybersecurity reaches a greater profile and there is more attention paid to and we understand the nature of the threat. There could be an overcorrection or an over response and I think to protect against that, we need to find measurable goals and milestones against those goals.

Could you talk about how Department of Homeland Security has defined those so far or plans to in the future?

Ms. LUTE. So when we speak about and everybody is searching for the illusive analogy in the physical world to cyberspace. You know, is it—is it like a global commons, you know, is it like clean air or clean water? I think cyberspace is more like light than air and I think it presents challenges in that respect.

What we want and what we have been promoting is an open, interoperable, reliable, and secure internet globally. Certainly that requires more than we can do in the Department of Homeland Security, more than we can do as a country, it requires all of us around the world. We have benefited enormously from this.

Our job in homeland security is to secure dot-gov and to work with the private sector to secure the Nation's critical infrastructure. We are evolving standards of what that means, reducing the number of attacks and threats, repairing instantaneously vulnerabilities as they are automated or as they are detected on an automated basis. So this will be an evolving set of challenges and issues that we will be dealing with.

Mr. O'ROURKE. What are the protections to the taxpayer with these evolving goals and definitions? I mean we can spend $10 billion, $100 billion, a trillion, $10 trillion, how do we know that we have spent enough, that our money is being used effectively, that we are meeting the goals that you and the oversight committee have agreed upon?

Ms. LUTE. Right. How do we know that what we are doing is working? If we have a removable media policy, is that enough? If we control access to our networks, is that enough? If we give everybody dual-key authentication responsibilities when engaging in networks, will that be enough? This is what we are crafting. We are doing it together with the private sector.

Because while we have ideas of our own, we know that they do as well. We look forward to working with this committee, because we know that you have ideas. So that is very much on our minds. Because we are determined to address this problem.

Mr. O'ROURKE. So you are talking about the process which you will undertake to define those goals and measure success and effectiveness. Are those specific goals, perhaps specific to the threats and challenges that we face in these, the three domains that you mentioned? Are those goals that you will share with this committee?

Ms. LUTE. Yes, absolutely.

Mr. O'ROURKE. We will be able to measure progress against those goals. Measure the effectiveness of the dollar spent.

Ms. LUTE. That is the, again, we operate on a duty-to-share model, in terms of information and how we work in Homeland Security. Especially in cybersecurity. So we will.

Mr. O'ROURKE. One of the things that you mentioned that caught my attention is cyber space is civilian space. There have been a couple of questions to this, but how do you see your job in terms of managing that balance that you talked about, between civil rights as you talked about it, personal freedom, liberties, the things that make the internet such a driver of economic growth and creativity in our country and in the world, and balance that against these security concerns?

Ms. LUTE. So if I could be permitted an example? I was the lead negotiator for the United States with the European Union on a data-sharing agreement called Passenger Name Recognition, PNR, to ensure the safety of air travel. It took us 18 months to have this negotiation. At the center of it was our ability to enforce our laws at our borders and to ensure the operational safety of the traveling public. Equally at the center was the role, were issues of privacy and civil rights and civil liberties.

We have been managing billions of files of data over the past 10 years in the Department of Homeland Security with respect to this traveling information. There has not been one privacy incident. So we think we can get it right. Again, I am an operator and this comes down to what it is we do.

Mr. O'ROURKE. That is impressive. Thank you. Thank you, Mr. Chairman.

Chairman MCCAUL. The gentleman, the gentlelady from Indiana, Mrs. Brooks, is recognized.

Mrs. BROOKS. Thank you, Mr. Chairman and thank you deputy secretary for being here and for your service. In 2012, FEMA and DHS held a National-level exercise. I have been a deputy mayor in the city of Indianapolis in the late 1990s working closely with public safety. As a U.S. attorney have worked with Federal, State, and local on a number of exercises, particularly after 9/11. I value the importance of exercises. It was on the Nation's ability to prevent, respond, and recover from a significant cyber incident, as I understand it. We hear that obviously cyber incidents are becoming greater in number and in severity.

My question is: What role does FEMA play, before, during and after, a significant or a catastrophic cyber incident? At what point might we expect that, if that after-action report is finished, and if it is not finished, when can we expect its release?

Ms. LUTE. I will have to get back to you on the release of the after-action report. In my background and tradition, those are extremely important exercises, the lessons learned. What you want to do successfully in any organization, and we particularly want to do in Homeland Security, is embed these lessons learned so that we can replicate our success and avoid repeating failure.

Lessons learned are an important part of that. You know when I was a young Signal Officer in the Army, we use to do exercise all the time. The Signal Officer always had to keep everything running so that the infantry or armor, they could do exercises. But we had to have everything working perfectly. Well, what if it doesn't work perfectly? What are the consequences to our ability to operate? So how do you bake that in to our exercises and our understanding?

FEMA of course plays a key role in leading Federal-level exercises, which State and locals are so much a part. So we are beginning to bake this into our thinking about exercise scenarios. But also, FEMA also, you know, in the Department of Homeland Security, is the Federal Response Agency. So what are the consequences, how do we understand, working with industry, the consequences of catastrophic failure and what that will mean for the public? How do we mitigate it, how do we restore services quickly? Address our responsibilities in that regard. So very much on our minds.

Mrs. BROOKS. Does DHS, does FEMA actually possess the legal resources and authority it needs, in the case of a catastrophic incident?

Ms. LUTE. Well FEMA certainly has the authorities that it needs to respond to an incident. What we know is that, a cyber incident could have consequences that matter for which FEMA is appropriately authorized to respond.

Mrs. BROOKS. Okay. Do you know how FEMA works with the private sector in, I am not certain, are you familiar with the exercise that they did in 2012?

Ms. LUTE. Yes, yes.

Mrs. BROOKS. How does FEMA work with the private sector in recovery?

Ms. LUTE. Well, well again, you know one of the things about Homeland Security is our partnership with the American people. FEMA is an example of where we live that every day in response to disasters. So it is a very close working relationship. Our dialogue at the State and local level with FEMA representatives on the ground, with community leaders, political officials as well, it is pretty interwoven.

I think the central point for me on cyber and FEMA is that physical and cyber infrastructure are inextricably linked. There can be vulnerability to that infrastructure through cyber, to which we have to be attentive, broaden our minds and understandings of what could result, and mobilize the appropriate levels at the Federal level to respond. The appropriate resources at the Federal level to respond.

I would be happy to get you, to discuss this in greater detail. We are working with FEMA on the lessons learned, as you mentioned. We know that there could be consequences that we have to be attentive to.

Mrs. BROOKS. So how does FEMA interact with the other DHS components during a cyber incident specifically?

Ms. LUTE. They are at the table, appropriately, again for what response they may have to mobilize. The actions that they may have to take. They are certainly in the room and part of the response. As we understand the consequences of an event that may give rise to physical effects that would engage FEMA's responsibilities.

Mrs. BROOKS. Thank you, I yield back.

Chairman MCCAUL. Thank you. The Chairman now recognizes the gentleman from Nevada, Mr. Horsford.

Mr. HORSFORD. Thank you, Mr. Chairman and thank you, Deputy Secretary. It is been very informative to have you here in the presentation. I do have a specific question on cybersecurity but before I do that, while I have such a high-ranking representative, I wanted to share something with you and see if you could help me with the response.

I heard from one of our local veterans recently. His name is James Courtney. He served three tours in Iraq and he is disabled after 15 years of active duty in the United States Army. His wife and the mother of three U.S. citizens, all boys, does not have a green card. As I understand it, in 2003, Sharon was held by the Border Patrol for several hours and denied even a phone call to her family in El Paso. Without any explanation Sharon was told if she just signed a simple document, that she would be let go. She now stands accused of falsely claiming to be a U.S. citizen.

What do we say to families like this? Who have been affected by what is a broken process? From what I have heard, it sounds like this family has been wronged. Do you agree? What is the Department doing to address issues like this one?

Ms. LUTE. Congressman I am not familiar with the incident that you are speaking about. I don't want to give you an off-the-cuff answer. I would be happy to take the facts back as you represent them, and find out.

Mr. HORSFORD. If you wouldn't mind doing that. I know that this did occur in the prior administration and it is, some time ago but there are details that I think are important for this committee and for me to be able to respond to.

You know, Mr. Chairman, I think that as we address larger issues, other issues including immigration, it is these type of circumstances that I hope will be brought forward and I that we can also talk about.

Let me switch to the issue of cybersecurity. I wanted to follow up to the Ranking Member's question dealing with the sequester. You know, we have all agreed here today that cybersecurity is very important and that we need to work in a bipartisan manner to pass legislation to help both the private sector as well as the public sector.

But we have a sequester that is affecting our ability to do our job today. So I would like to understand what the impact of the sequester has been to your Department, specifically as it relates to cybersecurity.

Ms. LUTE. Thank you for that. Cybersecurity is not immune from the impact of sequester. Both our perimeter deployment Einstein E3A will be affected. Our ability to automate the continuous diagnostics and monitoring system will be affected as well. Our ability to reach out to stakeholders as well.

It is particularly important because in cyber space, in the world of technology, the problems and the solutions that we are going to be dealing with 2 years from now, haven't been invented yet. So this is a place and an environment where speed takes on a whole new meaning.

Mr. HORSFORD. As it pertains to the workforce because as we have heard from members in the private sector, this is a very specialized workforce, and as we develop information-sharing capacity, what is our ability to recruit and retain on the Department side, the skill set of the workforce that we need in this regard?

Ms. LUTE. Of course it is affected, as you know. But one of the things that we are doing is overhauling our whole approach to become a world-class home to a world-class cybersecurity workforce. By hiring, testing, and training to the highest standards of cybersecurity. These really are cyber ninjas. Those are the standards that we want to instill, train to, certify, and maintain. We want to attract folks. We want to open the pipeline with industry and with academia. We want to strategically manage this workforce across the Department, and indeed, across the Federal Government one day.

We want to overhaul our acquisition and procurement, including our workforce, so that they are as skilled of the needs in the contracting environment for this. We want to create a cyber reserve. So we are not standing still on this question at all.

Mr. HORSFORD. Just if I could ask if the Department could provide us the college initiatives, I guess, that you have done. If you could maybe share that information with those of us who want to make sure that the Department is doing everything it can to reach out to the next generation of graduates that we need.

Thank you, Mr. Chairman.

Chairman MCCAUL. Thank you. The gentlelady from New York, the Ranking Member of the Cybersecurity, Infrastructure Protection, amd Security Techonologies Subcommittee, Ms. Clarke is recognized.

Ms. CLARKE. Thank you, Mr. Chairman. Deputy Secretary Lute, I don't mind sharing you with Congressman Payne. I am the New Yorker here.

Let me first of all thank you for your passion, your talent, your expertise that you brought to bear on the cybersecurity mission for the Department of Homeland Security. It is truly refreshing.

I also want to extend a thank you to our Ranking Member, Mr. Thompson, for his leadership and partnership in penning the letter to Chairman McCaul and me regarding the legislative jurisdiction issues that threatens to undermine the DHS mission and marginalize the effectiveness of governance and oversight of this committee. I think it is really important that we not get into a bidding war, but we all play a very critical role in this new governance in this space.

Mr. Chairman, last year our committee faced strict resistance to legislating a strong statutory role for the Department of Homeland Security's cybersecurity mission. Though you may have differences of opinion with Mr. Lungren's legislation, the precise act, I am sure you would agree, that the strong authorities for the Department of Homeland Security were commendable.

Unfortunately, some colleagues last year were unwilling to consider giving DHS the statutory certainty that it sorely needs and prevented the legislation from reaching the floor.

So I am glad that you are holding this hearing today to hopefully spotlight the good work, and you have been, that the Department is doing. Just last month, ICS–CERT was awarded the best security team award at the RSA by "SC Magazine." I would like to insert that recognition into the record. I think that we need to—morale is important here.

Chairman MCCAUL. I agree and without objection, so ordered.

[The information follows:]

BEST SECURITY TEAM GOLD WINNER

The Industrial Control Systems Cyber Emergency Response Team (ICS–CERT) Security Team responds to incidents, vulnerabilities, and threats that can impact those industrial control systems (ICS) which operate critical infrastructure across the United States. These systems are vital for the processes used throughout many critical sectors that the Nation depends on every day.

The ICS–CERT Security Team's mission is to reduce cybersecurity risks by offering four core products and services to the Nation's critical infrastructure sectors: Providing situational awareness to Government and the private sector through National alerts and advisories that warn of cyber threats and vulnerabilities; conducting technical analysis of malware, system vulnerabilities, and emerging exploits; performing cybersecurity incident response for asset owners and operators; and partnering with the control system community to coordinate risk management efforts and serve as the focal point for information exchange.

The ICS–CERT Security Team has received National and international recognition as an essential element for coordinating cybersecurity risk reduction efforts among the Nation's critical infrastructure asset owners. Through its incident response, situational awareness, and recommended practices efforts, the team is recognized as a National resource for cybersecurity guidance.

It is also a key functional element of the DHS National Cyber Security and Communications Integration Center (NCCIC) and is integral to the Department's capability to coordinate National-level cyber events. ICS–CERT Security Team presence in the NCCIC Operations Center provides synergistic information-sharing value to the various public and private-sector partners participants.

http://awards.scmagazine.com/best-security-team-0

Ms. CLARKE. Thank you, sir.

I firmly believe that DHS's role needs the clarity and authority of statute to most effectively do its mission. That is why last year I introduced the Identifying Cybersecurity Risks to Critical Infrastructure Act to get an important segment of DHS's authorities written into law.

So Deputy Secretary Lute, can you talk about the importance of getting your Department's cybersecurity mission and authorities codified in statute? What aspects of DHS's cybersecurity mission do you think would be particularly impactful if we could fully authorize them?

Let me repeat that for you—can you speak to the importance of getting your Department's cybersecurity mission and authorities codified? What aspects of DHS's cybersecurity mission do you think would be particularly impactful?

Ms. LUTE. I certainly agree with the importance of that and the Secretary absolutely agrees. We think it is important in this rapidly unfolding field to clarify the responsibilities that this Department will be given, particularly when it comes to securing dot-gov, in the area of information sharing as well.

Ms. CLARKE. With that, I yield back the balance of my time.

Chairman MCCAUL. Well, I thank you for your questioning. Know that I am committed to getting this done, to getting existing authorities codified, and to making the Department as strong a player as they are in this very important field, working together with the other agencies. I think we have one last Member, the gentleman from California, Mr. Swalwell.

Mr. SWALWELL. My district is in Northern California and it includes northern Silicon Valley and it is really the cradle of innovation. We also have two National laboratories and, I believe, more Ph.D.s in our district than anywhere else in the country. Very smart, innovative folks in our district, and I am concerned that if we were to get hit hard in our district, we would fall hard.

I am also concerned that if we sneezed from a cyber attack, the rest of the country could catch a cold because of the ripple effect of what it would mean to many of the industries in our district. We are talking all of Silicon Valley south and then, of course, the part of Silicon Valley that is in my district in the north.

So I am concerned that right now the rest of the country also does not understand enough about what the real threat is here. I want to know what we can do to better educate. Because we are starting to hear more about the threat, but—and folks, I think, will accept that their computer may get hacked. Someone may send out an e-mail in their name that didn't come from them.

But I don't know if we are prepared yet or we understand that we could go to the bank one day and our account balance could say zero. Or we could show up to work one day and our job is no longer there because the technology or something critical to the employer has been stolen by someone abroad.

When I was a prosecutor for 7 years, I worked closely with telecommunication companies to prosecute a number of our homicide cases, to work with them on subpoena compliance as well as ways to make sure that it was a two-way street, that their cooperation would not mean they would be penalized for working with us.

Now I know that we do have the National Cybersecurity and Communications Integration Center and my first question is what is the participation like, in that center, with private industry and what can we do, legislation-wise and as far as coordination efforts, to make sure that private industry is really working with us?

Because I know from being a prosecutor that it has to be a two-way street and because 90 percent of the networks are not dot-gov or dot-mil, if we don't have their cooperation or participation, we can't truly protect against the threat.

Ms. LUTE. Well, thank you for the question and thank you for your part of the country. I took my Ph.D. from Stanford. I am a believer. I am a believer.

It is an extraordinary National asset for us, the vibrancy and the contribution of that community, not only to this country but to the world. This instantaneous organic growth of the internet, in many ways can trace its lineage back to this part of the country. We certainly appreciate it.

We also appreciate the role of collaboration in the private sector. I speak very often with the leadership of private industry out in the Valley. They are extraordinarily thoughtful on all of the questions that we have discussed today.

On the NCCIC thought, to your specific question, we do have private industry representatives in some of the various sectors and we can talk to you in detail about that. For those members, Mr. Chairman, who have yet to come see us, we invite—that door—let me just reiterate your invitation and urging that they come and see us.

We agree on the partnership. We agree on the two-way street. We agree on the need for collaboration. We are putting our money where our mouth is in terms of having them on the floor with us at an operational level and including dialogue with them at a policy level at my and the Secretary's—in our discussions with them as well.

So across the board I agree with you.

Mr. SWALWELL. Great. Right now in this era of sequester, and we don't know how long this is going to last, but we do know that the threats are going up and the money to fight the threats are going down. How much does that concern you that your budget could continue to be on the chopping block and reduced as our country becomes more and more vulnerable to a cyber attack?

Ms. LUTE. Nothing is standing still. As I mentioned before, in cyber space, the problems and the opportunities that even 2 years from now, perhaps even 1 year from now, that we will be dealing with have not been invented yet. So time is of the essence.

Mr. SWALWELL. Finally, as a prosecutor, it is frustrating to me that it seems like we spend most of our time defending against the threat, but it is very hard, and I understand from the cases I have had, it is very hard to go after somebody on the law enforcement side and prosecute an individual who is hacking against us, tracing where the individual is coming from, which oftentimes is across the world.

Can we truly, really not just prevent the threat or prevent a cyber attack, can we truly go after an individual and prosecute them and hold them to account?

Ms. LUTE. I am a big fan of the rule of law and I am a big fan of the power of the law in this country. We are working very closely with the FBI to strengthen the hand of law enforcement. We have mentioned this is one of the things that we think cyber legislation would usefully add, which are tools to put them in the hands of law enforcement officers to successfully prosecute cyber criminals.

Mr. SWALWELL. Great. Thank you, Mr. Chairman.

Chairman MCCAUL. Thank you. Let me say, Deputy Secretary Lute, let me thank you for your testimony. It is been very impressive and I think very productive towards our discussions in developing legislation, which as I state, is a high priority.

Also, Chairman Meehan and I will be scheduling tours for our members to the NCCIC and we look forward to seeing you out there again.

With that, I know the Members will have—they have additional questions. You need to—you should respond in writing. With that, the clerk will prepare the witness table for the second panel.

Okay, with that, let me go ahead and introduce the next panel and thank you for your patience.

First we have Mr. Anish Bhimani; he is the managing director and chief information risk officer, JPMorgan Chase and is chairman of the Financial Services Information Sharing and Analysis Center, also known as the FSISAC, industry-wide organization charged with facilitating information sharing among the various members of the financial services sector as well as Government agencies. He has served as chairman since 2011 and on the board since 2009.

Next we have Mr. Gary Hayes; he is the vice president and chief information officer at CenterPoint Energy. In this position he oversees the information technology infrastructure and systems for the company's electric and gas delivery services, some actually in my district. Mr. Hayes has decades of experience in the field of energy infrastructure protection.

Thank you for being here today.

Last we have Ms. Michelle Richardson; she is the legislative counsel with the American Civil Liberties Union where she focuses on National security and Government transparency issues. Before joining the ACLU, Ms. Richardson served as counsel to the House Judiciary Committee where she specialized in National security and civil rights.

We look forward to hearing from all of you. Your full statements will appear in the record, and I would also like to note that Mr. Dean Garfield, CEO of the IT Industry Counsel was also scheduled to appear but had a scheduling conflict. I ask unanimous consent that his statement be entered into the record.

Without objection, so ordered.

[The information follows:]

PREPARED STATEMENT OF DEAN C. GARFIELD

MARCH 13, 2013

Chairman McCaul, Ranking Member Thompson, and Members of the committee, thank you for the opportunity to testify today. I am Dean Garfield, president and CEO of the Information Technology Industry Council (ITI), and am pleased to testify before the House Committee on Homeland Security on the important topic of cybersecurity. ITI represents global leaders in innovation, from all corners of the information and communications technology sector, including hardware, software, and services.

You have asked ITI to speak on the topic of cyber threat information sharing. Within that context, I would like to focus my testimony today on three areas: (1)

The opportunity facing the United States to establish a cybersecurity policy framework that is a model for the rest of the world; (2) the critical role of bidirectional industry-Government information sharing in a robust cybersecurity policy framework; and (3) key considerations regarding how U.S. civilian agencies can effectively contribute to effective information sharing.

OUR OPPORTUNITY: THE RIGHT CYBERSECURITY POLICY FRAMEWORK

I want to begin by stating a fact I think all of us agree on: We all are committed to protecting the Nation from cyber threats. The tech sector, other industries and stakeholders, Federal and State governments—we share a common responsibility to work collaboratively to provide effective, forward-thinking strategies and solutions that safeguard the American people and the networks and systems upon which we all rely. For us in the tech sector, this responsibility is part of our ethos. It is built into every one of our products and services.

During the past few years, both Congress and the administration, working with numerous private-sector stakeholders, have sought to create policies to improve America's cybersecurity posture, particularly critical infrastructure (CI) cybersecurity. We commend the efforts our policymakers have devoted to the unique challenge of better protecting America's citizens, critical assets, and infrastructures from ever-evolving cyber threats.

ITI and our member companies have been deeply involved in the policymaking process. Our views are based on a comprehensive set of cybersecurity principles for industry and Government we developed to better inform the public cybersecurity discussion.[1] ITI's six principles aim to provide a useful and important lens through which any efforts to improve cybersecurity should be viewed. To be effective, efforts to enhance cybersecurity should:

(1) Leverage public-private partnerships and build upon existing initiatives and resource commitments;

(2) Reflect the borderless, interconnected, and global nature of today's cyber environment;

(3) Be able to adapt rapidly to emerging threats, technologies, and business models;

(4) Be based on effective risk management;

(5) Focus on raising public awareness; and

(6) More directly focus on bad actors and their threats.

We were pleased the cybersecurity bills passed by the House last year—on cybersecurity R&D, cybercrime, education and awareness, information sharing, and others—embodied these principles. We understand many of the ideas Members of Congress are contemplating this year will enable these approaches. We are also appreciative that the President's recent Executive Order adopts these same principles. Overall, the United States appears to be embracing a cyber environment that encourages efficiency, innovation, and economic prosperity while promoting security, business and individual privacy, and civil liberties.

The United States is, however, not the only country grappling with how to develop the right cybersecurity framework. Governments around the world are also wrestling with important questions of how to protect their citizens and businesses in the face of ever-evolving cyber threats. Unfortunately, the approaches some other governments are taking do not always put innovation and collaboration first. Some governments are enacting inflexible, heavy-handed cybersecurity-related laws and policies that are rooted in top-down regulation and technology mandates. Most worryingly, these mandates are country-specific and thus at odds with global best practices. Such approaches rarely provide better security and in many cases may weaken security and disrupt global commerce and innovation.

Thus, the U.S. approach is important for an additional reason. We can and must set a good example for the rest of the world about the right way to approach cybersecurity policy. And as we execute on our approach, it will be important that we in both Government and industry collaborate with our peers around the world to tackle our shared challenge. Cyberspace is a global and interconnected domain that spans geographic borders and National jurisdictions. Top-down approaches being pursued in other nations undermine the greater global collaboration that is needed to respond to threats. The U.S. Government must proactively seek dialogues with our trading partners about how to achieve the requisite levels of security needed to meet National security concerns while preserving interoperability, openness, and economic development.

---

[1] *http://www.itic.org/dotAsset/191e377f-b458-4e3d-aced-e856a9b3aebe.pdf.*

THE ROLE OF BI-DIRECTIONAL INDUSTRY-GOVERNMENT INFORMATION SHARING

Mr. Chairman, Mr. Ranking Member, effective sharing of actionable information among and between the public and private sectors on cyber threats, and incidents is an essential component of improving cybersecurity. To be as nimble and flexible as many cyber intruders are, we need an improved information-sharing system that operates in real time, ensures protection of personal data, and is bi-directional—from the private sector to Government, and from Government to the private sector. Of course, effective information sharing itself is not the goal. What matters is the action relevant stakeholders take with that shared information to manage and mitigate cyber risk. But we know from experience that, once effectively informed of the specific threats they face, organizations take appropriate and reasonable measures to mitigate them.

Although many public and private-sector entities participate in information-sharing activities, there is broad agreement that gaps exist. ITI has worked closely with policymakers over the past few years, providing ideas and possible solutions for what types of improvements could and should be made. Overall, our recommendations fall into four general areas.

First, we should improve upon existing information-sharing organizations rather than create new structures. We need to better leverage our current organizations and evolve them into more effective partnerships for true sharing. Dozens of organizations and structures play important roles facilitating cybersecurity information sharing among private entities and between the private and public sectors. Some key examples include the Information Sharing and Analysis Centers (ISACs), the U.S. Computer Emergency Readiness Team (US–CERT), and the National Cybersecurity and Communications Integration Center (NCCIC). These and other organizations represent nearly all sectors of the economy as well as Federal, State, and local governments.

Second, we must improve the flow of actionable information from Government to industry. Government has unique insight into certain types of threats or hazards. When provided with this insight, the private sector's ability to assess risks, make prudent security investments, and develop appropriate resiliency strategies is greatly enhanced. The Executive Order intends to improve the Government's sharing of actionable information with the private sector on specific, targeted cyber threats and technical indicators that flag risks generally. We hope these changes are executed quickly, but we also believe that more needs to be done legislatively to build on the Executive Order.

Third, we must address liability concerns that impede information flows. Private entities holding information about cybersecurity risks often decline to voluntarily disclose it, or delay disclosure, for fear of lawsuits or regulatory actions. There is a need for limited safe harbors in these cases, and this is a key role for Congress. We look forward to also working with you to pass legislation in this regard.

Finally, privacy must be protected while information sharing is increased. We believe effective cybersecurity should strengthen personal privacy. For that reason, a policy framework must ensure that information that companies might share with the Government and each other for cybersecurity purposes should only be used for those purposes. This will protect civil liberties and at the same time give companies confidence that what they share will not be used for unrelated, unintended purposes.

THE WAY FORWARD: THE ROLE OF U.S. CIVILIAN AGENCIES

As we work to improve Government-industry information sharing, ITI understands policymakers are thinking about how the U.S. Government can better coordinate and execute its roles and responsibilities vis-á-vis the private sector in this area. Civilian agency leadership in this regard is critically important. ITI believes that whatever agency has principal responsibility for cybersecurity information sharing coordination should follow three key tenets. First, the lead agency needs to build on existing Government resources so as not to create new redundancies and confusion. Second, those tasked with this job must have the technical proficiencies to be able to provide rapid, real-time, situational awareness. Finally, the lead agency must ensure Government-wide respect for the legitimate data security, privacy, and civil liberties concerns I alluded to earlier.

CONCLUSION

Mr. Chairman, Mr. Ranking Member, ITI and our member companies are pleased you are continuing to consider how we can improve information sharing for the purposes of cybersecurity. We stand ready to provide you any additional input and assistance. In addition to this testimony, we are submitting for the record two ITI papers that provide more detailed recommendations on how information sharing can be improved.[2] Thank you.

The Chairman now recognizes Mr. Bhimani for 5 minutes for his opening statement.

STATEMENT OF ANISH B. BHIMANI, CHAIRMAN, FINANCIAL SERVICES INFORMATION SHARING AND ANALYSIS CENTER

Mr. BHIMANI. Thank you, Mr. Chairman.

Chairman McCaul, Ranking Member Thompson, Members of the committee, my name is Anish Bhimani and I am appearing today as the chairman of the Financial Services Information Sharing and Analysis Center, FSISAC.

The FSISAC was established in 1999 in response to Presidential Decision Directive 63. It is a nonprofit organization funded entirely by its member firms and sponsors. Its membership is comprised of over 4,400 financial and banking institutions, large and small, and it serves as a primary industry forum for collaboration on the critical cybersecurity threats facing the financial sector.

Despite the competitive nature of our industry, members of the FSISAC recognize that the threat from cyber attacks affects all of us. That defending the Nation's critical infrastructure is not a competitive issue.

To effectively combat this threat, we must come together as a sector and leverage the full capabilities of our collective membership. Above all, the key to the success of the FSISAC is trust amongst its members. Trust is not something that can be mandated nor easily earned.

Indeed, over the past 14 years, FSISAC members have worked tirelessly to engender trust amongst each other and promote the flow of threat information across the sector. These efforts have paid off significantly.

In January of this year, members of the FSISAC shared over 92,000 pieces of threat intelligence and approximately 400 events across the sector.

Equally critical is a strong partnership and close collaboration with Government agencies. One example of this partnership is the successful effort to obtain over 250 secret-level clearances and several top-secret SCI clearances for key financial services personnel. These clearances have enabled FSISAC members to receive briefings on new security threats and implement defenses to combat these threats.

We would like to see this process updated and expanded to provide more clearances to the private sector and make it easier for this information to be shared more broadly and quickly with our members.

Another good example of partnership is the work of the National Cybersecurity and Communications Integration Center, NCCIC at DHS, of what we heard said earlier.

Since June 2011, FSISAC representatives cleared at the top-secret SCI level have attended NCCIC daily briefs and other meet-

---

[2] ITI Recommendation: Steps to Facilitate More Effective Information Sharing to Improve Cybersecurity (October 2011), and ITI Recommendation: Addressing Liability Concerns Impeding More Effective Cybersecurity Information Sharing (January 2012).

ings to share information on threats and potential impacts to the sector. Our presence on the NCCIC floor has greatly enhanced the sector's awareness of and ability to respond to continuously evolving threats against the industry.

In 2011, a pilot program known as the Government Information Sharing Framework, or GISF, was launched with the Defense Department. Under the program, an initial 16 financial services firms were granted access to advanced analysis on cyber threats. The GISF provided an invaluable service of the sector, enabling participants to receive actionable and timely information that allow them to search for similar activity in their own environments. Unfortunately, the Department of Defense terminated the pilot program in December 2011 due to funding limitations.

The FSISAC strongly supports not only restarting the GISF program or a program like it, but also expanding its reach across the entire financial services sector.

In addition to our DHS partnerships, we also benefit tremendously from having a strong sector-specific agency, specifically, the Treasury's Office of Critical Infrastructure Protection plays an invaluable role to the sector serving as a conduit between our members and the various agencies that play a role in critical infrastructure protection. We believe that given its knowledge of the industry, as well as its relationship with various agencies, Treasury is uniquely qualified to serve in that role.

Finally, I would like to point out that it is impossible to discuss information sharing without also considering what specific information we need to share in order to most effectively protect our infrastructure.

Although much of the current debate around information sharing has focused on the very important goal of protecting privacy, we believe that much could be accomplished without ever sharing any personal information. The most valuable information we could gain, such as technical details of cyber attacks, analysis of incident attack patterns, techniques and trends and contextual information about threat actor groups and campaigns tends to be extremely technical in nature and doesn't necessarily need to include any personal information nor reveal the organization affected.

Whatever information we receive, the most important thing is that it be actionable and timely. Cyber threats are coming out as faster than ever before and are growing increasingly complex. As a result, receiving stale and outdated information is of very little value. In fact, it is a drain on resources and a waste of valuable time.

We are strong advocates of a framework where our respective agencies and companies can deliver relevant information very quickly at network speed with information flowing in both directions.

In closing, please accept my thanks on behalf of the FSISAC for the opportunity to address the committee on this critical issue. The ability to share information across the sector as well as our partners in Government and law enforcement, while still protecting privacy and civil liberties is core to our industry and our Nation's response of the growing threat.

I look forward to any questions the committee may have.

49

[The prepared statement of Mr. Bhimani follows:]

PREPARED STATEMENT OF ANISH B. BHIMANI

MARCH 13, 2013

Chairman McCaul, Ranking Member Thompson, and Members of the committee, my name is Anish Bhimani, and I am the chief information risk officer of JPMorgan Chase & Co. I am appearing today as the chair of the Financial Services Information Sharing and Analysis Center (FS–ISAC). I thank you for the opportunity to address the committee on the important topic of roles and responsibilities of the Government and private sector in the critical area of cybersecurity.

I would like to address a few points today: First, an overview of the FS–ISAC, its charter, purpose, and membership; lessons learned with regard to information sharing; perspectives on the FS–ISAC membership's interaction with Government agencies; and finally, recommendations around information sharing and cybersecurity governance.

FS–ISAC BACKGROUND

The FS–ISAC was established in 1999 in response to Presidential Decision Directive 63. This directive, later updated by Homeland Security Presidential Directive 7, required public and private-sector organizations to share information about cyber threats and vulnerabilities, with the goal of helping protect the Nation's critical infrastructure. The FS–ISAC is a nonprofit organization funded entirely by its member firms and sponsors. Its membership is comprised of thousands of financial and banking institutions, large and small, and its mission is straightforward—to provide the primary industry forum for collaboration on the critical cybersecurity threats facing the financial services sector. From 12 founding members at its inception, the FS–ISAC has grown to over 4,400 organizations, including commercial banks and credit unions of all sizes, brokerage firms, insurance companies, exchanges and clearing houses, payments processors, and over 30 trade associations, representing the majority of the U.S. financial services sector.

The overall objective of the FS–ISAC is to provide the financial services sector with the information it needs to defend against cyber threats and risk. It acts as a trusted third party that allows members to share threat, vulnerability, and incident information in a timely, trusted, and, if desired, anonymous manner. FS–ISAC information-sharing services and activities include:
- Delivery of timely, relevant, and actionable alerts from various sources distributed through the FS–ISAC Security Operations Center (SOC);
- Trusted mechanisms to facilitate member sharing of threat, vulnerability, and incident information, in either an attributed or non-attributed manner;
- Sector-specific groups and subcommittees that provide forums for members in a given part of the sector, e.g., the Payment Processors Information Sharing Council (PPISC), Insurance Risk Council, Payments Risk Council, Community Institutions Council, and the Clearing House and Exchange Forum (CHEF);
- Bi-weekly threat information sharing calls for members and invited security/risk experts to discuss the latest threats, vulnerabilities, and incidents affecting the sector;
- Engagement with private-security companies to identify threat information of relevance to the membership and the sector;
- Development of risk mitigation best practices, threat viewpoints and toolkits, as well as member-driven research regarding best practices at member organizations;
- Subject Matter Expert committees, including the Threat Intelligence and Business Resilience Committees, which provide in-depth analysis of risks to the sector, and provide technical, business, and operational impact assessments, as well as strategies to mitigate risk; and
- Participation in sector, cross-sector, and National exercises and drills, such as the Cyber Attacks Against Payment Processes (CAPP), National Level Exercise 2012, and the Cyber Storm series.

Despite the competitive nature of our industry, members of the FS–ISAC recognize that the threat from cyber attacks affects all of us, and that defending the Nation's critical infrastructure is not a competitive issue. We all recognize that to effectively combat this threat, we must come together as a sector and leverage the full capabilities of our collective membership. We also know that we must trust one another. Trust, simply put, is the key to the success of the FS–ISAC, and any information-sharing model.

Trust is not something that can be mandated, nor easily earned. Indeed, over the past 14 years, FS–ISAC members have worked tirelessly to engender trust amongst each other and are using all of the capabilities listed above to promote the flow of threat information across the sector. As an example, the FS–ISAC has built a model for sharing information in an authenticated, but anonymous, manner for those organizations that wish to take advantage of it. In addition, we have instituted a "traffic light" protocol, indicating levels of information sensitivity and how information may be disseminated to the membership, partners, and other organizations. These mechanisms have effectively and efficiently enabled the amount of information shared among FS–ISAC members to grow from a mere trickle a few years ago, to a veritable (but manageable) flood today. In January 2013, members shared over 92,000 pieces of threat intelligence and approximately 400 events across the sector.

U.S. GOVERNMENT INTERACTION

Equally critical as industry collaboration is our partnership with Government agencies. We could not protect ourselves against cyber attacks without extremely close collaboration, partnership, and most importantly, information sharing, with a number of Government agencies—most notably, the U.S. Department of Treasury and the Department of Homeland Security, but also the Federal Reserve, Office of the Comptroller of the Currency, United States Secret Service, U.S. Cyber Command, Federal Bureau of Investigation, National Security Agency, Central Intelligence Agency, and State and local governments. Additionally, the FS–ISAC is a member of, and partner to, the Financial Services Sector Coordinating Council (FSSCC) for Homeland Security and Critical Infrastructure Protection, established under HSPD7, and works extremely closely with the Financial and Banking Information Infrastructure Committee (FBIIC), under the auspices of the President's Working Group on Financial Markets. These organizations and relationships are part of the financial sector's long history of public-private partnership with various Government agencies in the area of cybersecurity.

One example of this partnership is the successful effort by the Department of Treasury, Homeland Security, FBI, U.S. Secret Service, and other partners to obtain over 250 secret-level clearances and several TS/SCI clearances for key financial services sector personnel. These clearances have enabled FS–ISAC members to receive briefings on new security threats and have provided useful information to the sector to implement effective controls and defenses to combat these threats. We know that this process is not always easy, and that sponsoring private-sector clearances has, historically, been difficult. But in our view, given how much cyber information is classified, it is absolutely essential that private-sector representatives have access to this information. The FS–ISAC would like to see this process updated and expanded to provide more clearances to the private sector, and make it easier for this information to be shared more broadly and quickly with our members.

Another good example of partnership is the work of the National Cybersecurity & Communications Integration Center (NCCIC) at DHS. In June 2011, the FS–ISAC became the fourth private-sector organization to place staff on the floor at the NCCIC. Specifically, FS–ISAC representatives, cleared at the Top Secret/SCI level, attend NCCIC daily briefs and other meetings to share information on threats, vulnerabilities, incidents, and potential impacts to the sector. These individuals interact on a daily basis with the NCCIC, routinely submit and respond to requests for information, collaborate on analyses and work with the NCCIC staff to determine what information from the NCCIC would be of use to our members, and what can be shared with whom. Over the past 18 months in particular, our presence on the NCCIC floor has greatly enhanced situational awareness and information sharing between the sector and the Government, as well as across other critical infrastructure sectors that participate on the floor. More recently, the FS–ISAC has embedded a full-time staff person on the NCCIC floor in addition to the part-time resources that were deployed last year.

One of the high points in the public-private partnership with the sector occurred in 2011 when a pilot program, known as the Government Information Sharing Framework (GISF) was launched with the Defense Department. Under the program, an initial 16 financial services firms (with a plan to expand participation later) were granted access to advanced threat information, as well as to classified analysis on threat actors and mitigation techniques. The GISF provided an invaluable service to the sector, enabling the pilot participants to receive actionable, timely, and contextual information that allowed them to search for similar threat activity in their own environments. It also allowed private-sector participants to adjust their assessments of cyber espionage threats using intelligence that had previously been unavailable. The program jump-started new efforts across the industry and helped re-shape the sector's approach to assessing cyber espionage risks.

Unfortunately, the Department of Defense terminated the pilot program in December 2011 due to funding limitations. The GISF was a significant leap forward in the public-private partnership, and represented a critical line of defense in mitigating the growing cyber threat. The loss of that information feed has already been felt, as numerous financial institutions have experienced activity from actors first identified through GISF reporting and intelligence. The FS–ISAC strongly supports not only restarting the GISF program, but also expanding its reach across the financial services sector. We urge Congress and the Department of Defense to resolve any outstanding funding or authorization issues and reinstate this crucial program.

As you can see, the financial services sector, and the FS–ISAC in particular, work in collaboration with a wide range of Government agencies—probably more than anyone would imagine. At the same time, we benefit from having a strong sector-specific agency—the Treasury Department—that allows us to navigate the various Government agencies involved in cybersecurity.

Specifically, the Treasury's Office of Critical Infrastructure Protection plays an invaluable role to the sector, serving as a conduit between our members and the various Government agencies that play a role in critical infrastructure protection. We believe that, given its knowledge of the financial services industry, as well as its relationship with various intelligence agencies, Treasury is uniquely qualified to serve in that role. Regardless of which organization is involved, however, the key is that we receive timely, actionable data from the appropriate source, whoever that is, so that we can take the appropriate action.

CREATING A USEFUL INFORMATION SHARING FRAMEWORK

There are two critical elements to creating a useful information-sharing framework: Determining what information should be shared, and developing robust processes for sharing timely information.

In thinking through this problem, it is impossible to construct an effective information-sharing framework without also considering what specific information we need to share to most effectively protect our infrastructure. Although much of the current debate around information sharing has focused on the important goal of protecting personal information, we believe that much could be accomplished without ever sharing personally identifiable information. With that in mind, here are a few examples of information we at FS–ISAC believe would be most helpful to share:
- Technical details of cyber attacks as seen on networks, in IT systems, or by victims, including IP addresses of attackers and their networks;
- Analytic content of incidents, attack patterns, and trends without revealing the organization affected;
- Analysis of technical details to determine the techniques, tools, and procedures that adversaries are using to target victim organizations;
- Contextual information about threat actor groups and campaigns;
- Information about the motivation, objectives, and capabilities of these groups or campaigns.

In addition to those most critical data elements we think must be shared, we also believe that critical infrastructure owners and operators would benefit from having a much stronger framework around how we share.

The cybersecurity threats the financial industry faces are coming at us faster than ever before, and are growing increasingly complex. As a result, receiving stale and outdated information is of very little value in protecting our infrastructure—in fact, it is a drain on resources, and a waste of valuable time. We are strong advocates of a framework where our respective agencies and companies can deliver relevant information very quickly, at network speed, with that information flowing in both directions.

Why is that important? Today, we in the private sector face attacks that were once directed only against major Government institutions. Government agencies may have established strategies and tactics to deal with those attacks that would be valuable to those us facing similar threats. Likewise, the financial sector has collectively established strategies and tactics that may be of use to Government agencies. Sharing these strategies and tools to deal with advanced threats comprehensively and quickly would do a great deal to help us all fight advanced attackers.

CONCLUSION

In closing, please accept my thanks on behalf of the FS–ISAC for the opportunity to address the committee on this critical issue. The risks associated with cyber attacks and threats are real, and of paramount importance to the financial industry as a whole. The ability to share information across the sector, as well as with our partners in Government and law enforcement, while still protecting privacy and civil liberties, is core to our industry and our Nation's response to the growing threat.

I look forward to any questions the committee may have.

Chairman MCCAUL. Thank you, Mr. Bhimani.

The Chairman now recognizes Mr. Hayes for his testimony.

STATEMENT OF GARY W. HAYES, CHIEF INFORMATION OFFICER, CENTERPOINT ENERGY

Mr. HAYES. Thank you Chairman McCaul, Ranking Member Thompson, and Members of the committee. My name is Gary Hayes, I am the chief information officer for CenterPoint Energy and thank you for inviting me to testify and share my experiences and perspectives on cybersecurity and our Nation's critical infrastructure.

A few quick points about CenterPoint Energy, we are headquartered in Houston, Texas. We have electric transmission and distribution, natural gas distribution and interstate pipeline. We serve over 5 million metered customers, primarily in Arkansas, Louisiana, Minnesota, Mississippi, Oklahoma, and Texas.

In other words, we are the owner/operators of multiple critical infrastructure systems. We take cybersecurity seriously.

As identified in our enterprise risk management program is one of the highest corporate risk. We have been in the cyber business for well over 10 years. The issue is the game has changed. The volume, voracity, and variety presented by extremely sophisticated and organized bad actors whose intent is to steal information or impact operations continues to exponentially evolve.

The question is: How do we work together to meet these dynamic and ever-changing and evolving threats?

I strive to keep my team focused by reminding them we need excellent solutions quickly not perfect solutions eventually. We have to keep that same thought in mind.

Some key takeaways that I would like for us to talk about. First, we need shared goals and collaboration. Excellent solutions for collaboration, information sharing, and technology sharing. It is very clear we need each other in this cyber war, situational awareness, information, tools, and techniques to be proactive and not reactive.

We must have a peer-to-peer partnership built on those shared goals, objectives, and trust to achieve these results.

The good news is there are some examples of this today. Our industry's collective cybersecurity work with the DHS, DOE, TSA, and NIAC provides a foundation but we need more.

Second, we need a pragmatic cyber framework. A framework must be based on the principles of risk and agility, a framework that provides value. It must provide learning, strategies, objectives, techniques, and tools that can be aligned with that risk.

Another challenge is there is energy providers from hundreds of customers to millions of customers. So our solution has to be scalable. A one-size-fits-all will be ineffective and costly.

Finally, we must have incident readiness. The reality is advanced persistent threat actors are not going away and the risk of cyber incidents remain. Increased situational awareness coupled with joint response and recovery plans have to be incorporated into everyone's current operating procedures.

As I mentioned before, the effort in the electric sector with NIAC is an excellent example of an emerging Government and industry effort to address resiliency and incident response.

In closing, I grew up in Oklahoma right in the heart of Tornado Alley. Any time a large thunderstorm rolled across the plains, my mom had us in the cellar. My dad stood at the top of the stairs looking at the sky trying to see if a funnel cloud was forming. Sometimes we were there for hours.

Now flash forward a few decades, today we have tremendous situational awareness, meteorology based on advances in technology tell us when the funnel is forming. How strong is the tornado? What is the path and the time that it is going to reach our location? Couple this with education of the public, improvements and construction techniques and emergency response plans and we dramatically changed tornado safety.

Looking back, I realize my parents were being responsive to the best information they had. The risk of not acting was too great.

Today, I feel I am standing at the top of the cellar stairs looking to the skies and watching for that cyber tornado. We have protection in place but constant vigilance is our mission in this cyber storm. In summary, we must join in shared goals, peer-to-peer collaboration to be proactive and to be prepared.

Chairman McCaul, Ranking Member Thompson, and Members of the committee, we appreciate the opportunity to share our perspectives and stand ready to assist you in your efforts as you move forward to protect our critical infrastructure.

[The prepared statement of Mr. Hayes follows:]

PREPARED STATEMENT OF GARY W. HAYES

MARCH 13, 2013

OVERVIEW

Chairman McCaul, Ranking Member Thompson, and Members of the committee, my name is Gary Hayes and I am the chief information officer for CenterPoint Energy. Thank you for inviting me to testify on my experiences and perspectives on protecting critical infrastructure from cyber attacks.

CenterPoint Energy, Inc. ("CenterPoint Energy"), headquartered in Houston, Texas, is a domestic energy delivery company that includes electric transmission and distribution, natural gas local distribution, natural gas gathering and processing, interstate pipelines, and competitive natural gas sales and services. It has assets totaling more than $21 billion. Our company has approximately 8,800 employees and serves more than 5 million metered customers primarily in Arkansas, Louisiana, Minnesota, Mississippi, Oklahoma, and Texas.

As the CIO of CenterPoint Energy I am accountable for our cybersecurity programs and have direct responsibility for our corporate business systems' cybersecurity. Because of the diverse segments of the energy infrastructure in which CenterPoint Energy's companies participate, I coordinate, collaborate, and communicate with our operational technology functions to define policies, procedures, practices and programs in our efforts to provide cybersecurity. I have a highly dedicated, educated, and capable team executing responsibilities in this effort.

I also have the responsibility to represent and coordinate representation of our company in industry and Government efforts focused on cybersecurity.

We focus heavily on participation in relevant industry groups. I participate on the American Gas Association ("AGA") and Edison Electric Institute ("EEI") Cyber Task Groups and I coordinate with David Jewell, senior vice president, Commercial Operations, Optimization and Gas System, who represents CenterPoint Energy on the Cyber Task Group for the Interstate Natural Gas Association of America ("INGAA").

We also participate in numerous governmental, private, and industry-related efforts focused on cybersecurity.

Our cybersecurity technologies operate across three areas: Interstate pipelines, local gas distribution utilities, and an electric utility. For cybersecurity purposes, our interstate natural gas transmission pipelines are under the jurisdiction of the Transportation Security Administration ("TSA"). Our local gas distribution companies operate under the same jurisdiction but, for cybersecurity purposes, have no single regulator because some of the Federal authority has been delegated to the States. And, finally, CenterPoint Energy's electric utility in the Houston, operates under the jurisdiction of the Federal Energy Regulatory Commission ("FERC") for compliance with North American Electric Corporation reliability standards. We also work voluntarily with a multitude of other groups including the Federal Bureau of Investigation, Industrial Controls Systems Cyber Emergency Response Team (ICS–CERT) and the Department of Energy (DOE) and, of course, Department of Homeland Security (DHS).

My goal today is to share CenterPoint Energy's perspective with regards to cybersecurity challenges, activities, and opportunities. That perspective is this: Cyber threats are evolving and require collaboration, information sharing with the Government, and continued collaboration with the industry to effectively protect the Nation's critical infrastructure. Our goal is to focus our resources on facing the cyber threat.

This perspective is shaped by our experiences and participation in industry groups as well as our collaboration with several Governmental agencies including the DOE, DHS, and the TSA. Furthermore, our relationship with members of our supply chain, our suppliers and vendors, is critical. From these experiences, we have determined that we need the ability to respond in a quick and agile manner, as well as continuously improve our capabilities to respond. Collaboration is the key.

As a critical energy transporter and distributor to the Nation, we know that we have responsibilities to the public, our customers, and our shareholders. We have prioritized our cybersecurity efforts in parallel with our corporate philosophy.

(1) Public Safety
(2) Energy Delivery
(3) Customer Service

I hope this document provides a helpful "participant's view and perspective" as we work together to protect our company and our Nation's critical infrastructure.

CYBERSECURITY EFFORTS AND COLLABORATION

CenterPoint Energy has a long history of safe and reliable energy delivery to our customers. Our team members take pride in getting up every morning with this mission top of mind. To this point, we take protection of the public, our control systems, customer and employee information, critical infrastructure information, and intellectual property very seriously. Cybersecurity has been incorporated into our processes, procedures, and operations through various mechanisms over time. But, we do recognize that the current cyber environment has escalated beyond historical expectations and our efforts must and will continue to evolve in order to meet these dynamic and ever-evolving threats.

We have evolved from a strategy of "perimeter defense" (e.g., keep the bad actors out) to a strategy of "depth-in-defense" (recognition that technology system perimeters were susceptible to compromise, depth-in-defense provides increased reliance on detection and response mechanisms to address threats within the protection perimeter). We have established objectives, techniques, talent, and tools to assist us in our current efforts. We have also focused on educating our workforce, as they represent the first line of defense. However, we recognize our cybersecurity capabilities must continue to evolve. This recognition comes from education and collaboration with industry and Government. Our objectives are to mature and enhance our strategy and move to an "agile defense".[1] In particular, we will enhance our focus on the people, processes, and technologies that can be managed, monitored, tested, measured, and continuously improved.

As an important part of the energy delivery value chain, we are also enhancing resiliency, which is our ability to respond quickly to attacks and to maintain critical services. As we have learned through our participation in many of the cyber discus-

---

[1] An enhanced comprehensive security strategy referred to by NIST as "agile defense". Agile defense combines traditional perimeter, depth-in-defense, and depth-in-breadth, which is a planned, systematic set of multidisciplinary activities that seek to identify, manage, and reduce risk of exploitable vulnerabilities at every stage of the life cycle. Life cycle is the network that includes product design and development; manufacturing; packaging; assembly; system integration; distribution; operations; maintenance; and retirement.

sions, "bad actors will get in". It is not a matter of "if" but a matter of "when." Therefore, we continue to evolve our capability to respond and operate in a compromised state.

Identifying and coordinating with the right stakeholders is vital to that evolution.

First, we believe that participation with industry coalitions is critical. Our collaboration with fellow energy sector members allows us to continually learn and incorporate leading practices, provide mutual assistance and educate stakeholders and policy makers of real risks and possible solutions. We encourage and assist in collaboration between AGA, EEI, INGAA, and key policymakers.

Second, collaboration between the public and private sector is a vital part of cyber protection. Deployment of the SmartGrid in Houston presented us with the opportunity to work with DOE, DHS, and other Federal agencies in order to successfully deliver advanced metering capabilities. Throughout the process, we collaborated with Government stakeholders to incorporate customer protection and cybersecurity into our design and operations. This could not have been achieved without information sharing, a focus on quality and integrity, strong risk management, and joint objectives—all of these achieved through collaboration.

Those partnerships are also critical for our intelligent grid project and we look forward to continuing those relationships.

Other examples illustrating the success of public-private partnerships are the joint industry and Governmental initiatives that developed the electric sector cybersecurity Capability Maturity Model, guidelines for the natural gas pipeline sectors' Pipeline Security Guidelines and many more activities that have benefited CenterPoint Energy and our industry. These collaborative efforts focused on targeted objectives and provided tangible programs, information, tools, techniques, and knowledge to help us enhance our efforts in this war against cyber threats. We encourage Congress to promote continued focus on private and public partnerships for the protection of our National security.

And, finally, cybersecurity collaboration must take into account the entire life cycle and supply chain. Therefore, we must recognize the essential participation of our vendors and suppliers in this effort. They have worked with us to provide products and solutions to meet the demands of this challenge. Our joint goals and efforts focus on design, testing, and improvement of products to understand quality, integrity, risks, threats, mitigations, and management of these solutions in our operating environment.

CYBERSECURITY PARTICIPANT OBSERVATIONS

There is a set of common themes that we see emerging from our cybersecurity efforts and dialogues:

Shared Goals.—Identifying and merging the focus and priorities of the stakeholders is a key to success.

Risk-Based Approach.—A risk-based approach is fundamental to our efforts. Goals should be prioritized and articulated clearly. Solutions should be focused and yet flexible. A "one-size-fits-all" approach won't work for unique problems. There are utility service providers serving hundreds of customers and others serving millions of customers; therefore, the risk profile will influence the objectives, techniques, and tools to effectively manage cybersecurity.

Information Sharing and Situational Awareness.—We desire a defined collaborative process to share information in a quick, secure, and non-prejudicial fashion. That process should educate us in ways that we can be proactive and not reactive. Throughout many conferences, meetings, calls, and other interactions, we continue to hear that the ICS–CERT serves as a strong template for developing a working model of collaboration. "Boots-on-the-ground" security team members find this of great value in their efforts in the cyber war. We believe this is an example of information sharing that provides actionable information, support to our industry, and brings value to public-private partnership.

Leveraging Tools and Techniques.—Although we, and many others, employ market-leading technologies and information solutions, we believe our effort would be greatly enhanced by leveraging cyber technologies and solutions utilized by Governmental organizations and fellow industry members. We recognize there are many obstacles, but today's cybersecurity challenges require us to remove these obstacles and provide a repeatable and supportable path to facilitate results. Each day of delay is another day of opportunity for advanced persistent threat actors.

Security Clearance.—Expanded security and expedited clearance for appropriate personnel within the private sector and expedited communication of critical information is critical to the ability of owners and operators to be proactive and responsive to emerging threats. We were pleased to see such a provision in the President's Executive Order on cybersecurity.

Cybersecurity Regime.—A cybersecurity framework must prioritize the principle that agility is the key to responding to cyber threats. An overly burdensome and prescriptive regulatory regime will be increasingly challenged to keep pace with evolving cyber threats. A beneficial framework not only defines capabilities, but provides learning, methodologies, objectives, and techniques (tools and measures) to achieve the required results. In conjunction with risk-based analysis, that type of framework can be leveraged by all participants to mitigate threats.

Incident Management.—The reality is advanced persistent threat actors are not going away and the risk of a cyber incident will remain top of mind for the foreseeable future. Increased situational awareness coupled with response and recovery plans will be incorporated into existing emergency operating procedures.

A leading effort on incident management comes under the auspices of the National Infrastructure Advisory Council (NIAC) report, several electric utility CEOs are engaged in an on-going partnership with the White House National Security Staff and senior officials throughout the Government, including Department of Energy Deputy Secretary Daniel Poneman and Department of Homeland Security Deputy Secretary Jane Holl Lute. This collaboration has resulted in several Government-industry initiatives, one of which is to identify roles and responsibilities that will expedite response and recovery should a major power disruption occur.

Collaboration.—All of these themes require partnerships with industry and Government. Collaboration is essential to our combined mission of protecting the public, customers, employees, critical infrastructure, intellectual property, and National security. Notable examples demonstrating the strength of collaboration between public and private sectors include the Industrial Control Systems Joint Work Group (ICS–JWG) and the TSA-sponsored public-private partnership which supports the National Infrastructure Protection Plan (NIPP).

To illustrate further, I offer the case of our interstate gas transmission pipelines where the cyber collaboration with the Federal Government began through our work with INGAA and AGA. After the September 11 attacks, and before the TSA or the DHS were created, we voluntarily collaborated through INGAA and AGA with the then-Research and Special Programs Administration within the Department of Transportation (DOT) to develop the initial Pipeline Security Information Circular. This collaborative approach to developing and implementing security measures continues to this day in our collaboration with the TSA. Since that time, gas pipeline owners and operators have worked with TSA to safeguard and protect our infrastructure's security—both from physical and cyber attacks. As a result of years of work and collaboration between owners and operators and the TSA we have a strong, trust-based collaboration—a public-private partnership. This approach, and the relationship it fostered, produced robust, thorough cyber guideline development for natural gas transmission pipelines even before the "911 Act" became law.[2]

TSA is using a voluntary partnership approach because it works. TSA and the private sector partner in order to leverage the collective expertise and experience of the Government and private industry in finding practical solutions to cybersecurity. This approach and the relationship it has fostered have produced robust cybersecurity guidelines and best practices for natural gas transmission pipelines.

The TSA approach builds on what has been proven through experience: Public-private partnerships for cybersecurity generate solutions. A Congressional Research Service August 2012 report, "Pipeline Cyber Security: Federal Policy," stated that "TSA officials assert that security regulations could be counter-productive because they could establish a general standard below the level of security already in place at many pipeline companies based on their company-specific security assessments." Moreover, the report notes that "[b]ecause TSA believes the most critical U.S. pipeline systems generally meet or exceed industry security guidance, the agency believes it achieves better security with voluntary guidelines, and maintains a more cooperative and collaborative relationship with its industry partners as well."

We believe that the key to effective cybersecurity is the trust developed in partnerships like the one with TSA. The dynamic solutions that are born of the public and private sector coming together are not possible when the Government is only acting as a regulator and enforcer. The cybersecurity world moves too quickly for such traditional regulatory models to be beneficial or productive.

---

[2] Implementing Recommendations of the 9/11 Commission Act.

CONCLUSION

We take seriously the responsibility of protecting our customers, employees, assets, and communities in which we operate, and thus cybersecurity is a top priority for CenterPoint Energy. We also recognize the importance of critical infrastructure to our National security. Because cyber threats are constantly changing and evolving, we support voluntary programs that encourage partnership, collaboration, sharing of information and technology, and the preparedness necessary to mitigate and respond to the ever-changing nature of cyber attacks. We will not succeed in this effort alone. The strengthening and expansion of industry and Government partnerships provides our best front in this cyber war.

Chairman McCaul, Ranking Member Thompson, and Members of the committee, we appreciate the opportunity to share our perspectives and stand ready to assist you in your efforts to protect our critical infrastructure.

Chairman MCCAUL. Thank you, Mr. Hayes. I appreciate your analogy. It is well taken.

Now the Chairman now recognizes Ms. Richardson for her testimony.

STATEMENT OF MICHELLE RICHARDSON, LEGISLATIVE COUNSEL, AMERICAN CIVIL LIBERTIES UNION

Ms. RICHARDSON. Chairman McCaul, Ranking Member Thompson, thank you for the opportunity to testify today on the Department of Homeland Security's role in cybersecurity.

This hearing is very timely. DHS is currently running major cybersecurity programs in order to secure critical infrastructure and Congress will likely vote on legislation further defining its role in the coming months.

One of the most important decisions Congress will make is whether domestic cybersecurity programs will remain in the hands of civilian agencies, like DHS, or be ceded to the military. Under long-standing American legal requirements and policy traditions, the military is restricted from targeting Americans on American soil.

Yet some are now arguing that cybersecurity should be the exception and the National Security Agency should be empowered to collect more information about internet users in order to respond to on-line threats. Doing so would create a significant new threat to Americans' privacy and must be avoided.

The NSA has developed extraordinary powers and has been granted incredible legal leeway, all under the premise that its spying would be turned outward against foreign enemies. Setting it free to collect American information for cybersecurity would be unprecedented.

This warning seems dire but that is because the consequences are dire. If domestic cybersecurity programs are ceded to the NSA, this committee, rank-and-file Members of Congress and the American public will never hear of it again. Keeping cybersecurity within DHS and within the jurisdiction of this committee would enhance privacy and accountability in very concrete ways.

In addition to being a bad deal for privacy, placing new programs outside of DHS isn't even necessary from a security perspective. The highest ranks of the intelligence community agree that DHS should retain authority over civilian cyber programs.

NSA Director Alexander has stated that his agency should not be the public face of domestic cybersecurity and that DHS should be the entity to deal directly with civilians, the private sector, and the domestic internet.

The Obama administration continues to empower DHS and other civilian agencies to pursue cybersecurity for critical infrastructure in the public. The other panelists discussed in their statements the many different existing programs and information sharing hubs that are working successfully through DHS and other agencies.

Its involvement in this area is only going to grow in light of the recent Executive Order. For example, the much-touted Defense Industrial Base Pilot Program, now known as the Enhanced Cybersecurity Program, will be expanded to all critical infrastructure and run by DHS. That program will organize and facilitate the flow of information from the Government to critical infrastructure.

Also under the Executive Order, DHS will conduct the first interagency privacy analysis of cyber information sharing. As noted by the other panelists, there are dozens of information-sharing bodies within and outside of the Government, all sharing different data pursuant to different statutes. No one has ever reviewed those programs for their effect on privacy.

The President endorsed the Fair Information Privacy Principles and that heartens us, and we look forward to DHS's public report, due back next year. This committee could help bring pressure to bear on the agencies in its jurisdiction to ensure that they conduct a full and meaningful privacy analysis as part of that product.

Since civilian control is decidedly better for privacy, works from a security perspective, and is already being implemented through current programs, it is disappointing that a legislative proposal that would fundamentally alter this balance is being considered.

The Cyber Intelligence Sharing and Protection Act, known as CISPA, would create a cybersecurity exception to all privacy laws, so that companies can share Americans' internet data with each other and with the Government, even in the absence of a warrant, subpoena, or emergency, and share that information directly with military agencies like the NSA.

In its veto threat, the administration argued this bill, "effectively treats domestic cybersecurity as an intelligence activity and thus significantly departs from long-standing efforts to treat the internet and cyber space as civilian spheres."

We hope the House will refer that bill to this committee or that you will otherwise consider taking up legislation of your own.

Thank you for this opportunity to testify. We look forward to working with this committee going forward on DHS's role in cybersecurity.

[The prepared statement of Ms. Richardson follows:]

PREPARED STATEMENT OF MICHELLE RICHARDSON

MARCH 6, 2013

Good morning Chairman McCaul, Ranking Member Thompson, and Members of the committee. Thank you for the opportunity to testify on behalf of the American Civil Liberties Union (ACLU), its more than half-a-million members, countless additional activists and supporters, and 53 affiliates Nation-wide, about the role of the Department of Homeland Security (DHS) in protecting the cybersecurity of critical infrastructure.

The topic of today's hearing is very timely. DHS is currently the lead agency running major cyber programs on behalf of the Government and critical infrastructure, but Congress is considering establishing a new information-sharing regime that could collect cyber information notwithstanding any of the privacy laws currently protecting Americans' sensitive and personal data, and some proposals are unfortunately questioning the role of DHS. Most Americans would agree that the enhancement of on-line security is a worthy and appropriate goal for those vested with the responsibility for safeguarding the interests of all Americans. Protecting the right to internet privacy—a right with roots in our Constitutional principles opposing unreasonable search and seizure and assuring limited Government—is as critical a goal as enhancing on-line security, and DHS is the agency best positioned to handle such new authority in an effective and accountable manner. We look forward to working with this committee to ensure that these new cyber programs remain under civilian, rather than military control, and that Congress conducts extensive oversight of all DHS programs to ensure protection of privacy rights.

Cybersecurity programs can and must be run in accordance with the Constitution and American values.[1] The internet is an incredibly useful and empowering tool that enhances public knowledge, broadens the reach of our free speech rights, and eases and facilitates daily business and personal activities. As a result, internet data is rich in intimate details of our private and professional lives, such as where we go, with whom we associate, what we read, our religious faith, political leanings, financial status, mental and physical health, and more. Protecting privacy is necessary for the public to feel confident in continuing to engage with new and developing technology; any cybersecurity initiatives should make protecting that privacy a paramount goal.

Many existing and proposed cyber efforts do not threaten the privacy or civil liberties of every day internet users, and we urge this Congress and the administration to pursue those programs and to avoid alternative proposals that risk creating major new and unnecessary surveillance programs. Appropriate programs for Congressional or administrative action include those to secure Government and military networks, educate the public on hygiene issues, prosecute internet-based financial crimes, invest in research and development, secure the supply chain of hardware, and share targeted threat information with critical infrastructure.

I. THE IMPORTANCE OF KEEPING DOMESTIC CYBERSECURITY PROGRAMS WITHIN CIVILIAN AGENCIES

Under long-standing American legal requirements and policy traditions, the military is restricted from targeting Americans on American soil. Instead, domestic intelligence and law enforcement activities are run by civilian authorities. Some are now arguing that cybersecurity should be the exception, and that military agencies like the National Security Agency (NSA) should be empowered to collect more information about every-day American internet users in order to respond to on-line threats. Doing so would create a significant new threat to Americans' privacy, and must be avoided.

To date, the military vs. civilian debate has been skewed by the intense focus on cybersecurity threats posed by hostile foreign governments, or international terrorists, and the comparative inattention to threats unrelated to National security. While advanced persistent threats from foreign actors are real and require a multifaceted response from the Government, it does not follow that all cybersecurity incidents impacting domestic internet users should merit a military response. Even by intelligence community estimates, those dangers represent a small portion of the threats that affect American internet users. Malware, financial crimes, and other threats that do not rise to the level of international incidents make up the overwhelming majority of malicious conduct on the internet. The conflation of foreign spying and potential sabotage, with corporate espionage, everyday internet crime, political statements, and essentially prank behavior has inflated every internet malfeasance into a potential National disaster. This hyperbole is simply not factually accurate, and only serves to encourage policy decisions with serious privacy and civil liberties implications.[2]

Placing cyber programs under the jurisdiction of domestic civilian agencies like DHS has real and far more positive consequences for transparency and accountability. DHS's lead competition for cyber programs—the NSA—is a black hole of information. Programs housed there, like in the rest of the intelligence community, are not subject to any meaningful public oversight. The NSA's activities appear to

---

[1] The American Civil Liberties Union's letters to Congress, comments to Federal agencies, blogs, and other cybersecurity materials may be found at *http://www.aclu.org/cybersecurity*.

[2] See, for example, Howard Schmidt, *Price of Inaction Will Be Onerous*, NYT, Oct. 18, 2012, available at *http://www.nytimes.com/roomfordebate/2012/10/17/should-industry-face-more-cybersecurity-mandates/price-of-inaction-on-cybersecurity-will-be-the-greatest*.

be presumptively classified, and whatever oversight that takes place is cabined in the Intelligence Committees, which conduct most of their business behind closed doors.

One only need look to intelligence wiretapping for an example of the dangers posed if Congress hands control over domestic cybersecurity to the NSA. In 1978, Congress established the Foreign Intelligence Surveillance Act (FISA) to govern foreign intelligence electronic surveillance. Federal judges meeting in a secret court issued opinions interpreting Americans' Constitutional rights and developed a secret body of law that the American public has not been allowed to read. The extreme secrecy around such intelligence programs helped conceal a program of illegal and warrantless wiretapping for over 6 years. Congress eventually amended the FISA to permit this warrantless surveillance to continue, but included a sunset provision that was scheduled to expire at the end of last year. Congress reauthorized it without having a single open hearing with administration witnesses to explain how this expansive authority affects Americans' privacy. While some claim this evolution of expanded wiretapping as a success of the intelligence oversight process, it reflects the limits and consequences of housing these programs behind the intelligence wall.[3]

If cybersecurity—with a set of programs dominated by non-military and non-National security concerns—is ceded to the NSA, this committee, rank-and-file Members of Congress, and the American public will never hear of it again. Keeping cybersecurity within DHS and other civilian agencies, and within the jurisdiction of this committee would enhance, not harm, both security and privacy.

II. THE CURRENT ROLE OF THE DEPARTMENT OF HOMELAND SECURITY IN CYBERSECURITY

Developments over the last several years have rightly steered domestic programs into the DHS or other civilian agencies. In 2010, the Secretary of DHS and the director of the National Security Agency (NSA) signed an agreement that put DHS in charge of cybersecurity in the United States, with the NSA providing support and expertise.[4] The President's recent Executive Order 13636 continues this approach, putting DHS and the National Institute of Standards and Technology atop the domestic cyber hierarchy, with consultation from the Attorney General, the Privacy and Civil Liberties Oversight Board, and the Office of Management and Budget.[5] These major structural and policy commitments add to long-standing DHS programs that share information with companies and infrastructure operators, educate the public, and secure Government systems.

DHS's role in the collection, use, and dissemination of cybersecurity information has substantially grown over the last several years. With the recent Executive Order, its participation will expand again, especially in two areas. First, DHS will run the Enhanced Cybersecurity Services program and facilitate the sharing of threat indicators with critical infrastructure owners and operators.[6] Information sharing in this direction—from Government to private sector—has far fewer privacy implications than the reverse. It does however cement DHS' role in information sharing and publicly available Privacy Impact Assessments suggest that the agency is imposing meaningful privacy protections for the personally identifiable information (PII) coming into its possession. For example, PII is not maintained in a system of records, and therefore is not searchable by name or other identifiers, and information is not retained unless it is "directly relevant and necessary" to address a cyber threat.[7]

Second, DHS will coordinate a review of current information sharing programs to determine whether they meet the ideas in the Fair Information Practice Principles (FIPPs).[8] Currently, there is little publicly available information about what agen-

---

[3] The Supreme Court recently ruled in *Amnesty* v. *Clapper* that ACLU clients lacked standing to challenge the FISA Amendments Act of 2008, because they could not prove that surveillance of their communications under the act was "certainly impending," all but foreclosing meaningful judicial review of that statute's constitutionality.

[4] MEMORANDUM OF AGREEMENT BETWEEN THE DEPARTMENT OF HOMELAND SECURITY AND THE DEPARTMENT OF DEFENSE REGARDING CYBERSECURITY, September 27, 2010, available at *http://www.dhs.gov/xlibrary/assets/20101013-dod-dhs-cyber-moa.pdf*.

[5] Executive Order 13636, Improving Critical Infrastructure Cybersecurity, 78 Fed. Reg. 11739, February 12, 2013 [hereinafter Executive Order].

[6] Id. at 4(c).

[7] PRIVACY IMPACT ASSESSMENT FOR ENHANCED CYBERSECURITY SERVICES, January 16, 2013, available at *http://www.dhs.gov/sites/default/files/publications/privacy/privacy_pia_nppd_ecs_jan2013.pdf*, at 7.

[8] Executive Order at (5).

cies are currently doing with cybersecurity information and this annual report will be the first overarching review of these programs.

III. EMERGING DOMESTIC INFORMATION-SHARING PROGRAMS MUST BE RUN BY CIVILIAN AGENCIES SUCH AS DHS

Congress is considering a significant expansion of the Government's authority to collect cybersecurity information, and if the expansion moves forward, it is critical for civil liberties that they be run by civilian agencies such as DHS. H.R. 624, the Cyber Intelligence and Sharing Protection Act (CISPA), would exempt cybersecurity information sharing from all privacy laws and reverse decades of statutory protections for sensitive information like our communication, financial, and internet information. It would permit corporations to determine what information pertains to cybersecurity and allow them to share it with the Government—including military agencies like the NSA—and other corporations without making a reasonable effort to shield or scrub out personally identifiable information that is unnecessary to address the threat at hand. Companies would then be free to use Americans' sensitive private information as they see fit, and the Government could use it for certain reasons other than cybersecurity. When one of those reasons—National security—is wholly undefined, we are especially concerned that the military and intelligence agencies accessing that information would consider themselves to have free reign over such private records, under ever expanding arguments of what National security includes. These and other fundamental problems are why the ACLU continues to oppose CISPA.

One of the biggest problems with CISPA is that it does not require companies that participate in this new information sharing regime to work with civilian agencies, and instead allows them to share sensitive and personal information directly with the NSA and other military agencies. The bill's sponsors claim that American corporations insist on dealing with the NSA and may withhold this information from the Government altogether if directed to go elsewhere. This assertion does not stand up, especially considering that the companies in question are not part of the defense sector, and primarily offer services to the public and the private sector. Companies that actually have defense information are already permitted to participate in a NSA-run information regime, and other potentially targeted sectors can continue to work with the agencies that have long regulated them.

CISPA insists on giving the companies the authority to share domestic, civilian internet information directly with the NSA even though it neither wants nor needs it. NSA Director General Keith Alexander has stated that his agency should not be the public face of cybersecurity and does not need to directly receive domestic cyber information.[9] In fact, the House Intelligence bill is an outlier. The administration's Statement of Administration Policy on CISPA in the 112th Congress, said that the bill:

" . . . effectively treats domestic cybersecurity as an intelligence activity and thus, significantly departs from long-standing efforts to treat the internet and cyberspace as civilian spheres. The administration believes that a civilian agency—the Department of Homeland Security—must have a central role in domestic cybersecurity, including for conducting and overseeing the exchange of cybersecurity information with the private sector and with sector-specific Federal agencies."[10]

---

[9] Jennifer Martinez, *General: Nation Needs DHS Involved in Cybersecurity,* THE HILL, Oct. 21, 2012, available at *http://thehill.com/blogs/hillicon-valley/technology/259547-general-nation-needs-dhs-involved-in-cybersecurity-,* ("I see DHS as the entry point for working with industry," [General Keith] Alexander said at an event hosted by the Wilson Center and National Public Radio . . . Alexander stressed that protecting the Nation's critical infrastructure requires a team effort from the Government, including the involvement of DHS. "Where I sit, it's our job to help them be successful. I think they're taking the right steps and it's the right thing to do," Alexander said. "Our nation needs them to be in the middle of this."); Kim Zetter, *DHS, Not NSA Should Lead Cybersecurity, Pentagon Official Says,* WIRED, Mar. 1, 2012, available at *http://www.wired.com/threatlevel/2012/03/rsa-security-panel/* ("'Obviously, there are amazing resources at NSA, a lot of magic that goes on there,' said Eric Rosenbach, deputy assistant secretary of Defense for Cyber Policy in the Department of Defense. 'But it's almost certainly not the right approach for the United States of America to have a foreign intelligence focus on domestic networks, doing something that throughout history has been a domestic function.' Rosenbach, who was speaking at the RSA Security conference in San Francisco, was adamant that the DHS, a civilian agency, should take the lead for domestic cybersecurity, with the FBI taking a strong role as the country's domestic law enforcement agency.").

[10] OFFICE OF MANAGEMENT AND BUDGET, EXECUTIVE OFFICE OF THE PRESIDENT, STATEMENT OF ADMINISTRATION POLICY, H.R. 3523, CYBER INTELLIGENCE

Continued

The Senate's most recent information-sharing legislation, Title VII of the Cybersecurity Act of 2012, also made clear that cybersecurity information should only go to a civilian agency.[11] While a handful of amendments to CISPA passed on the House floor last year, none of them addressed this point. Members of the Intelligence and Homeland Security Committees filed amendments that would have required new domestic information sharing to be routed through civilian agencies, but they were not made in order and did not receive a vote.[12] The administration, the Senate, and the privacy community are in agreement that civilian control of these programs is not only good for civil liberties, but workable from a cyber and National security standpoint. CISPA stands alone in failing to follow this common wisdom.

IV. FURTHER AREAS FOR COMMITTEE OVERSIGHT OF DHS CYBERSECURITY

Because of the House's imminent efforts to expand information sharing and the importance of keeping those programs in civilian hands, this statement has focused on that proposal and how it fails from a civil liberties and privacy perspective. But we also urge this committee to undertake oversight activities of existing cybersecurity programs. In particular, we urge the committee to review the implementation of the EINSTEIN program, which works with providers to scan Government systems for known cyber threats. The last Privacy Impact Assessment on EINSTEIN was written in 2010 and there is little public information about the broader application of the program and the effectiveness of privacy requirements. The committee should also make sure that agencies are participating meaningfully in the FIPPs review discussed above so that DHS can do an overarching analysis of whether privacy is protected in current programs.

V. CONCLUSION

Thank you for the opportunity to share our views on cybersecurity and the role of DHS. The administration is giving DHS increasing responsibilities in this area and we hope that if information collection programs expand, they too are housed in DHS. We look forward to working with you on this and other civil liberties issues in the future.

Chairman MCCAUL. Thank you, Ms. Richardson. This committee is, again, committed to taking up legislation. I think you raised some valid points and concerns in terms of a civilian versus military space.

Let me start with Mr. Bhimani. Your sector has been perhaps one of the most successful stories in terms of working with DHS and protecting your critical infrastructure. Yet, has been under attack, as you know, by countries like Iran and others quite extensively.

Could you share with this committee your experiences with your sector's participation with the NCCIC and how that has worked for your industry?

Mr. BHIMANI. Yes. Thanks very much for that recognition. I think our Members obviously think that we should very seriously devote thousands of people towards this problem. But individually, you can only go so far.

So with all the challenges that maybe have been facing this sector, I shudder to think what it would have been like if we hadn't been sharing with each other and hadn't had that partnership with both Treasury and DHS.

SHARING AND PROTECTION ACT, April 25, 2012, available at *http://www.whitehouse.gov/ sites/default/files/omb/legislative/sap/112/saphr3523r_20120425.pdf*.

[11] S. 3414, The Cybersecurity Act of 2012, 112th Cong. (2012).

[12] CISPA amendments filed with the with the House Rules Committee are available at *http:// rules.house.gov/Legislation/legislationDetails.aspx?NewsID=812*. Amendment 19 by House Permanent Select Committee on Intelligence Member Representative Jan Schakowsky (D–IL) and amendment 21 by House Homeland Security Committee Ranking Member Bennie Thompson (D–MS) would have ensured that new sharing under CISPA would have gone to civilian agencies and DHS respectively.

I think our presence on the NCCIC floor has really sped that partnership significantly, being able to get information both from the NCCIC as well as from our members to the NCCIC.

Chairman MCCAUL. Would you recommend—would it be your recommendation—well, first of all, it has been successful for you, your relationship with DHS and the NCCIC, is that correct?

Mr. BHIMANI. Yes, it has. I think there is always ways to improve any sort of partnership, but it is—if I compare it with the relationship we had with various agencies years ago, it is light-years ahead.

Chairman MCCAUL. Would you recommend in getting full participation from the 16 ISECs out there to participate on the NCCIC floor? Would that be helpful?

Mr. BHIMANI. Yes. The same way I said that I think that we as a sector recognize that us individually really have responsibility for the whole sector, if you look at all those sectors, there is a tremendous amount of dependency from one sector onto another. We have as much dependency on the electricity sector, the telecom sector, as we do on each other, right.

So I do think that there is a certain—and with as much progress as we made within the sectors, not just financial, but otherwise, sharing with each other, I do think doing that would significantly enhance cross-sector sharing, yes.

Chairman MCCAUL. I think that is going to be one of the goals of this committee, is to get full participation from the private sector.

Mr. Hayes, you obviously represent the energy side of the house. Obviously, the Mandiant report out there talks about China targeting our energy sector. Can you tell us about your experience with DHS and the NCCIC and why that would be valuable to codify that relationship into law?

Mr. HAYES. Sir we have had a good relationship with DHS, primarily around the ICS–CERT. When I go to meetings within the industry group and talk to the boots-on-the-ground security people, it is probably one of the security organizations that they reference the most in terms of the benefit it brings to them.

In terms of the NCCIC, we are learning about that. We want to understand that capability around situational awareness. As I mentioned, it is better to see the storm coming, to deal with it than have to react to it after the fact.

So those are the things that our industry is working with. We are working also with NIAC through both DOE, NSA, DHS, and several others, to look at a response plan for our industry as we move forward.

Chairman MCCAUL. Well, that is good because we always talk about the electric grid and how shutting that down would potentially cause more damage than Sandy or other hurricanes, if done effectively.

Ms. Richardson, I wanted you to expand, as you correctly noted, that General Alexander, the director of NSA, sees DHS having an important role with cybersecurity, particularly, as he put it, being a civilian interface to the private sector. Can you explain to this committee why that civilian interface is so important?

Ms. RICHARDSON. Sure. A lot of the press around cybersecurity has really focused on foreign actors and attacks at a very high level on our defense information, corporate espionage.

But overwhelmingly, the cybersecurity programs that affect everyday Americans are about everyday cyber crime, insecure networks, things like that. Those do not merit a military response. They should be handled by civilian agencies and the capability has certainly been built up there.

We can certainly look over the last decade that, as the Government has expanded its intelligence authorities, once you go behind that intelligence curtain, there isn't oversight and there isn't accountability and it operates in almost complete secrecy, with even Members of the intelligence committees saying that they don't have basic information on how these programs are run.

We don't see that happening nearly as much in programs that are run under DHS and are presumptively public.

Chairman McCAUL. So do you believe that civilian authorities over, say, the dot-com and the critical infrastructures, as has been put forth by both President Bush and Obama, is the better route to go?

Ms. RICHARDSON. Absolutely. That doesn't necessarily detract from the NSA and Defense working in its own sphere. They have their own authorities and they will continue to build them out.

However, as we turn to the public internet that everyday Americans are using, it absolutely has to be controlled by civilian agencies like DHS.

Chairman McCAUL. We are trying—I was looking at that bubble chart earlier, just trying to figure out the roles between the—I believe they all have roles and there is plenty work for everybody. I think it is clearly defining these roles between the three agencies that is highly important. We need to get this right before we pass legislation.

On the issue of privacy, Chairman Meehan and I are looking for ways to ensure that privacy is protected under the Constitution. We have looked at the Executive Order language as a possible starting point.

I know that your group, the ACLU, for the most part has been supportive of the language, in terms of the adoption of the Fair Information Practice Principles for internal information sharing. Is that a fair statement?

Ms. RICHARDSON. Yes. We were very happy to see the Executive Order embrace the FIPs. They represent principles like transparency, accountability, minimization, control over your own information. Those should be the bedrock going forward for information-sharing programs.

Chairman McCAUL. Okay. Well, thank you very much. That is all I have for now. I now yield to the Ranking Member.

Mr. THOMPSON. Thank you very much, Mr. Chairman. I am most appreciative of having other people talk about cyber, other than just in a classified setting or some other kind of setting where we can't talk about it.

Well, that kind of puts a muzzle on Members of Congress from going forward and trying to do the right thing, because it is presented to us in a manner where we can't talk about it.

So for this hearing, it has allowed us to hear from not just DHS, but also people who either do it everyday or people who review policy everyday. What I would like to do for each one of our witnesses is to say we are not trying to reinvent the wheel. Most private sector businesses' best practice says we have to have a secure network as best we can.

We are not trying to create a bureaucracy on top of that, so no "you have to do it this way because the Government says to do it this way."

Now that being said, do I hear from the private sector that it is important for a civilian coordinating role to be part of this cybersecurity policy?

Mr. Hayes, we can start with you and we will go from there.

Mr. HAYES. Yes, I believe it is very important to have that clear role. I think there was the discussion earlier with Ms. Lute about the FEMA. We utilize the FEMA ICS formats in our structure, so clear command in incident situations are important.

It is also equally important as we work with our partnership and organizations across our industries and our agencies, that it is clear in how we are dealing with that. What information can be shared, what information can be shared openly, fairly, quickly, responsibly? Those are things that are very, extremely important to us, because those are the things we react to.

As my other speaker talked about, actionable items, how do we get to actionable items? That is what we do on a daily basis. So without the clarity of roles and responsibilities across those organizations, then we are providing multiple perspectives. Just to give you an idea, as we track the number of entities, and that could be Governmental or industry or whatever, we are well over 70 different groups that are focusing on cybersecurity. So as a single company, you can't support 70 types of activities. You have got to focus on the ones that are providing the value, creating the value, providing the information that you can respond to and actually benefit both your company and the customers that you serve.

Mr. THOMPSON. Mr. Bhimani.

Mr. BHIMANI. I do believe it is important to have a civilian agency involved. What I would say, just echoing Mr. Hayes's comments, is it is often difficult for those of us in the private sector to navigate the various agencies and departments involved in cybersecurity.

We have benefited tremendously in the financial industry from having the Treasury Department and their critical infrastructure protection office do that for us. So I strongly believe that there be a single organization to be that conduit. I think, the call-out of sector-specific agencies in the Presidential directive, I think is a step towards that.

I think, as I mentioned before, our partnerships with DHS have been very strong, both with the NCCIC as well as with the Intelligence and Analysis Directorate.

What I would say is what we care most about is that we are able to receive actionable, timely information from whoever has it, and not necessarily be limited to those agencies we can speak with as dictated by what we need.

Mr. THOMPSON. Ms. Richardson, I would say on top of that, how would the need for transparency and oversight impact perhaps what we have heard from these other two witnesses?

Ms. RICHARDSON. Well, I think often transparency, oversight, privacy are conceptualized as opposite to timely sharing and agility that is needed in this area. That is not necessarily the case.

There are ways to conduct information sharing that absolutely builds in all of the privacy principles that are so important to protect this very sensitive data. So it is very possible to do a very targeted information-sharing program that clearly defines what can be shared, who can receive it, and what can be done with it.

The answers to those questions are just technical data, stripped of the personal information, with civilian agencies who can then use it just for cybersecurity purposes. The devil will be in the details, but there is nothing inconsistent with providing these guys with what they need and doing it in a way that protects privacy.

Mr. THOMPSON. Thank you. I yield back, Mr. Chairman.

Chairman MCCAUL. Thank you.

The Chairman now recognizes the Chairman of the Cybersecurity, Infrastructure Protection, and Security Technologies Subcommittee, Mr. Meehan.

Mr. MEEHAN. Thank you, Mr. Chairman.

Thank you for this very distinguished panel taking the time not only to be before us today but for the work that you are doing out there in the private sector, in all matters of it.

Because as we have identified in numerous aspects of today's hearing, this is a true public-private partnership and in more ways than perhaps in any other in Government, because we are tied together so significantly. I look forward to working with you, each of you, as we move forward.

Mr. Bhimani, let me ask you a question because I think you touched on something that is important in my understanding. It is as much to educate those who are out there, taking very seriously the important points that have been made by Ms. Richardson and the recognition that you and I think the banking industry have for the security of private information and other kinds of things, a long history of being able to do that.

You spoke a little bit in your testimony about what may be necessary for you, and I think there are two points that I want you to speak to. It is necessary so it is real and actionable. But you also don't want to be getting a lot of information that as you, in your words, if it is stale it is a waste of time.

We also appreciate that a lot of times we are talking about fractions of seconds within which the speed of this game is moving before somebody can be violated.

So can you speak to a little bit more about what the nature of that information that you are looking for, how it can be actionable but yet at the same time not necessarily be identifiable in a way that would create concerns for people who might be the subjects of some of that?

Mr. BHIMANI. Sure, I would be happy to.

Let's go back to when we think about any sort of an attack, what do we care most about? We care most about the method of the attack, the nature of the attack and, frankly, the motivation of the attacker, right?

There is a term that we use a lot in cybersecurity, it is called an indicator of compromise, or an IOC. So sharing those indicators of compromise from one firm to another. Hey, we saw some activity from this address. Those sorts of things are very useful from that perspective.

One other example might be we——

Mr. MEEHAN. So it may not be—it is not necessarily content-specific?

Mr. BHIMANI. No.

Mr. MEEHAN. It is really—could you just talk for a second—like——

Mr. BHIMANI. Sure. Sure. So——

Mr. MEEHAN. So what is that information? Is it—or what?

Mr. BHIMANI. Yes, so it might be—yes, it might be an IP address. It might be a specific vulnerability in a system that was exploited. It might be——

Mr. MEEHAN. Back door, so to speak, or something like that?

Mr. BHIMANI. I am sorry?

Mr. MEEHAN. A back door, so to speak.

Mr. BHIMANI. A back door, so to speak, yes.

Mr. MEEHAN. We understand the soft way. This is the way it is being exploited.

Mr. BHIMANI. Exactly. So basically, what is the attack technique used around that, right? I think that, if I go back to something I mentioned before, the GISF, right? One of the things that was most valuable out of that was, look, we can't tell you why or where this is, but if you see something coming from this IP address, be worried. That is something you should block. That is the kind of stuff that we need, right? So what we don't need to do is—you know, back to this—a majority of what we need tends to be machine-level data, right, IP addresses, vulnerabilities in software, specific attack patterns or things like that, that have nothing to do with an individual's information or an individual's data.

In fact, in most cases, those things sit in two different systems within our organizations, right? So even by sharing one, you are almost physically barred in some cases from sharing the other one, because it comes from a completely different place.

Mr. MEEHAN. Well, thank you. This is an issue that I want to explore. I appreciate the points that have been made by Ms. Richardson, as well, and I think we are going to be looking to explore ways in which privacy can be protected, but we can be actionable in an appropriate fashion.

Just, Mr. Hayes, you represent not just the energy industry, but in my mind, the broad spectrum of kind-of, sort-of utilities and otherwise, so it could be water, it could be a whole variety of things. There is also sophistication that has been identified. Your industry, Mr. Bhimani's industry, are really at the cutting edge of this, but there is a lot of things, municipal water supplies. I mean, they are paid for by taxpayer, rate-payer dollars. They have got systems that are 20 and 30 years old. They are not built for the current level of cybersecurity.

How are we going to be able to include all of the important partners in this at the same time, you know, without creating or—you know, standards that become check the box or become problems in which we talked about clutter? It almost becomes counterproductive. I am interested in your observations on how we can encourage people to participate and at what point in time the relationship starts to become counterproductive, because it becomes overly bureaucratic.

Mr. HAYES. So I think it was hit on earlier about how we are integrated together, that all the systems are such that we touch each other and have dependencies. I mentioned earlier that, you know, there are companies—small municipal water facilities, small electric companies, rural electric cooperatives who may have one person in their IT department. How does that one person stay up with all of what is happening from that perspective?

It is going to have to look at a risk-based profile. Are their actions as necessary as perhaps the actions of a large utility serving millions of customers? They may be of equal consequence in some ways, but the overall major consequences that could occur may be different. So I think developing the skill sets and knowledge to do risk-based analysis helps us understand how to prioritize and focus those areas where we need to make the best investments.

Now, stepping away from that, we participate with organizations and industry groups in a variety of all sizes. Many of those will come to the seminars or the learning sessions, and if we learn, we share those best practices, and those people are willing to go back and incorporate those things within to their environments, within their risk profile, so I think it goes back to not only info sharing, information sharing, like we have talked about, but even within our industry groups, continuing to broaden the bigger footprint of thhe needs and necessities for information sharing in those areas.

Mr. MEEHAN. Well, thank you. Thank you for the work that you do, and look forward to working with you collectively in the time ahead to do what we can in this public-private partnership to get it right. Thanks.

Thank you, Mr. Chairman. I yield back.

Chairman MCCAUL. I thank you. Let me just, in closing, since we don't have any other Members asking questions, if I could just give each of you just a couple minutes to highlight the most important points as you see it and particularly as we move forward with legislation, what you believe to be the most important pieces to that legislation?

We will start with Mr. Bhimani.

Mr. BHIMANI. I would just echo—reiterate the importance of being able to get actionable, timely information out to the private sector from whatever the source, right? I do recognize a lot of the challenges between the civilian and the intelligence agencies, right? But at the end of the day, you know, we need to know what is going on and what is affecting us in a way that makes sense, so that is the first thing I would say.

The second thing I would say in conjunction with that is, just reiterating my earlier point that it can often be very difficult for private-sector entities to navigate the number of agencies and the number of departments within agencies that do this, so having a conduit, like in our case Treasury, to serve as that point of contact for the industry I think is invaluable.

Mr. MEEHAN. [Off mike.]

Mr. HAYES. I think what is necessary is for the clarity of roles. I know that was talked about a lot today, and I think that is very beneficial. Anything that considers that helps us understand how do we interact helps in that process.

It has got to be practical and immediate. This is a timely issue. The people and what we are dealing with are things that, as mentioned, need to be actionable. We need to come back and be able to do things and apply technologies and techniques and intelligence against solving this problem.

Risk-based, one-size-fits-all is not appropriate. We have got to think about how we can address that small municipal all the way up to the larger utility infrastructures. Timely—and it is going to be timely in the fact that, how do we move from being reactive to being proactive to being predictive? How do we get the game where we are understanding that we might see these things coming earlier, often referred to as situational awareness? The other one is scalable. So what we need to do is it goes to my point. We have got to be able to apply this across the spectrum of our industry so it is effective to all.

When we talk about legislation, just simply, it has got to be to where I don't have to go to my legal department or my regulatory department to address an issue. So if it creates those constructs— and I don't go and work in those constructs—but if it creates those constructs, it makes information sharing difficult, slows the process down. So keep that in mind as we move forward.

Last, it has got to be peer-to-peer and collaborative. We have talked about that throughout, and I heard that tremendously through the session, that is built on the trust that we both are going to react responsively in this effort to solve the problem around cybersecurity.

Chairman MCCAUL. Thank you.

Ms. Richardson.

Ms. RICHARDSON. Thank you. When we are evaluating cybersecurity legislation, we are very happy to report that largely it doesn't affect civil liberties, and there are a lot of things that the Government and Congress can be doing that are civil liberties-neutral, like building up capacity at DHS or education programs, research and development, securing the supply chain, and we really hope the Government will focus on those programs and not the ones that implicate civil liberties.

To the extent, though, that the Government does want to increase information sharing and write laws that are going to contravene long-standing privacy statutes, there are a couple of things that have to happen. No. 1, those programs have to be civilian-run and by an agency like DHS. No. 2, those programs have to minimize the collection of personally identifiable information. No. 3, those programs have to absolutely tamp down the use of that information once it is collected, so that it is not purposed for things outside of cybersecurity.

I think the last thing is just to urge you to take the time to get this right. I think we have seen that once the Government is formally given authority, it is almost impossible to get it back. So if Government now overreaches and allows too much information to be shared, I don't know how fixable it will be, so we hope that Congress makes sure that there is a very targeted, tailored approach going forward.

Chairman MCCAUL. This has been very insightful. I want to thank the witnesses for your testimony.

Pursuant to Committee Rule 7–E, the record will be held open for 10 days. Members may have additional questions in writing.

Without objection now, the committee stands adjourned.

[Whereupon, at 12:42 p.m., the committee was adjourned.]

APPENDIX

Question 1. Has the Department released the National Level Exercise 2012 After-Action Report? If not, when will the Department release the report?

Answer. The final National Level Exercise 2012 After-Action Report is currently in clearance and FEMA will provide a copy to Congress once it is approved. However, the NLE 12 Quick Look Report (attached) has been released and is publicly available.*

Question 2. Last year FEMA released the National Preparedness Report (NPR), which showed that significant gaps still remain in our Nation's Cybersecurity capability. The NPR reported that the Nation was not even half-way to the desired capability level for cybersecurity. What should we do to educate and train our Federal, State, local, and private-sector partners to help build and mature the Nation's cybersecurity capability?

Answer. Emerging cyber threats require the engagement of the entire Nation—from Government and law enforcement to the private sector and most importantly, the public. Raising the cyber education and awareness of the general public creates a more secure environment in which the private or financial information of individuals is better protected. DHS advocates for a safe and secure cyber environment by conducting outreach and awareness efforts to educate and inform the general public about cybersecurity opportunities to enhance their confidence to protect themselves on-line.

In 2011, DHS released the *Blueprint for a Secure Cyber Future,* which calls for a coordinated effort across the homeland security community to protect America's critical information infrastructure and build a safer and more secure cyber ecosystem. Such tools and resources that promote cybersecurity education include the DHS/NSA Centers for Academic Excellence, the CyberCorps Scholarship for Service Program, the Integrated Cybersecurity Education Communities Program, and the Federal Virtual Training Environment, which provides on-line access to cybersecurity training for State, local, territorial, and Tribal governments.

DHS recognizes that partnership and collaboration are crucial to ensuring that all Americans take responsibility for their actions on-line. To that end, we are continuing to grow the Department's public-private partnerships through the *Stop.Think.Connect.*™ Campaign, which is a year-round National public awareness effort designed to engage Americans and encourage them to join the effort to practice and promote safe on-line practices. In addition, National Cyber Security Awareness Month (NCSAM) is an opportunity to engage public and private-sector stakeholders—as well as the general public—to create a safe, secure, and resilient cyber environment.

The Department promotes cybersecurity in grades K–12 and higher education. Key programs provide established undergraduate and graduate specializations at designated universities and scholarships in exchange for Federal service after graduation. DHS, in coordination with the National Initiative for Cybersecurity Education, is currently institutionalizing and delivering tools and resources through the National Initiative for Cybersecurity Careers and Studies (NICCS) portal. The NICCS public website is a comprehensive on-line resource for cyber education and training for Federal employees and the general public.

DHS is building strong cybersecurity career paths within the Department and in partnership with other Government agencies. To accomplish this critical task, we have created a number of competitive scholarship, fellowship, and internship programs to attract top talent, including computer engineers, computer scientists, ana-

---

*The document has been retained in committee files and is available at *https:// www.llis.dhs.gov/sites/default/files/National%20Level%20Exercise%202012%20Quick%- 20Look%20Report.pdf.*

lysts, and IT specialists. For example, the Homeland Security Advisory Council Task Force on Cyber Skills provided recommendations in October 2012 that will help DHS develop the next generation cyber workforce. The Department has worked to fulfill recommendations that expand the National pipeline of men and women with advanced cybersecurity skills, enable DHS to become a preferred employer for the talent produced by that pipeline, and position the Department to help make the United States safer, more secure, and more resilient.

Finally, the Multi-State Information Sharing and Analysis Center (MS–ISAC) provides managed security services to States and local governments, education and training services, and resources to non-member SLTT governments on a fee-for-service provision and to the public. The MS–ISAC has since grown to include all 50 States, three U.S. territories, the District of Columbia, and more than 200 local governments.

In addition, the National Computer Forensic Institute has trained more than 1,000 State and local law enforcement officers since 2009 to conduct network intrusion and electronic crimes investigations and forensic functions. Several hundred prosecutors and judges as well as representatives from the private sector have also received training on the impact of network intrusion incident response, electronic crimes investigations, and computer forensics examinations.

Question 3. In February, the Emergency Alert System of two television stations in Montana was compromised and a fake emergency alert message warning of a zombie apocalypse occurring in several counties. While this incident did not cause any harm, my concern is that the American people rely on public information during crisis and disasters to help guide their actions and hacking into the system could cause great harm or confusion. What are some measures that can be taken to prevent this from occurring again and assure the American people the information we provide through the emergency alert system is accurate?

Answer. A Federal Communications Commission's (FCC) investigation of the false emergency alert messages identified several standard best practices that could have prevented this event. The FCC's review revealed that the broadcasters were using off-the-shelf technology, but had not acted on the manufacturer's recommendation to change the default password and user ID codes. The default user ID and passwords are contained in the manufacturer's on-line manual and are easily discoverable. In addition, critical portions of the broadcaster's network were accessible through the public internet and were not isolated by a firewall. The following security best practices, published by the National Association of Broadcasters, would greatly reduce the possibility of future similar events:

(1) Follow the manufacturer's installation instructions;

(2) Change manufacturer passwords immediately upon installation of the purchased equipment;

(3) Employ a strong password model (using combinations of letters, numbers, and symbols) that must be changed periodically; and

(4) Install firewall software to protect critical internal networks from easy public access.

Implementation of these basic security practices would help to prevent future abuses. Further, the National Protection and Programs Directorate/Office of Cybersecurity and Communications is engaging with the Federal Communications Commission and the Federal Emergency Management Agency to examine system configuration and recommending additional measures for consideration and implementation by manufacturers and broadcast system owners and operators to increase security and system integrity.

QUESTIONS FROM HONORABLE SCOTT PERRY FOR JANE HOLL LUTE

Question 1a. When a company from the private sector chooses to report that they fell victim to a cybersecurity crime, what is the process by which they go about doing that? Specifically, what is the department or agency they report to?

Answer. Successful response to dynamic cybersecurity crime requires leveraging homeland security, law enforcement, and military authorities and capabilities, which respectively promote domestic preparedness, criminal deterrence and investigation, and National defense. DHS, the Department of Justice (DOJ), and the Department of Defense (DOD) each play a key role in responding to cybersecurity crimes, with each department having areas with overlapping jurisdiction regarding law enforcement, protection, and response. Regardless of which agency receives an initial incident report, these Federal entities regularly share incident information in a manner that protects privacy and civil liberties, and coordinate on response activities such that "a call to one is a call to all."

Question 1b. If the Government substantiates the claim, what information can be provided to the company? Specifically, is the company given tools to prevent future attacks; do they receive the origin of the attack?

Answer. If a company requests that DHS evaluate a suspected intrusion, the company may voluntarily provide network or system log data to the NCCIC for technical review to ascertain the characteristics of an incident. The NCCIC will analyze the log data and provide the company with a detailed analysis, classified and/or unclassified as appropriate, and recommend mitigation strategies. Other agencies, like the FBI, may also coordinate with DHS to share information with the company.

The Department's enhanced cybersecurity and communications collaboration, situational awareness, and everyday response capabilities through the NCCIC allow for information sharing across all levels of government and the private sector for cyber incident situational awareness and coordinated response and recovery efforts. DHS routinely shares threat knowledge in anonymized, non-attributable formats, with the private sector to enable effective computer network defense during steady states as well as in response to a more particularized threat. In response to an incident, DHS frequently provides analysis to assist in mitigating the activity or preventing future attacks. In addition, the NCCIC shares timely and actionable incident data with the affected company as well as interagency partners and across multiple sectors to enable alert and warning activity, helping other partners protect themselves before they are impacted. For instance, the Cybersecurity Information Sharing and Collaboration Program allows for sharing and receiving anonymized actionable threat data: With participating private-sector entities that provides protection for information submitted and enables collaboration with other entities in response to cybersecurity threats and incidents.

DHS also offers a number of voluntary programs to increase an entity's cybersecurity posture upon request. These include the Cyber Security Evaluation Tool, which is a self-assessment tool downloadable from *www.us-cert.gov* and a library of recommended practices that a company can follow to increase their cybersecurity posture. Additionally, critical infrastructure owners and operators can request an on-site Cyber Resilience Review of their organization's overall cyber posture or an assessment of their control systems' security from the Industrial Control Systems Cyber Computer Emergency Response Team.

Question 2. Currently, it is in the best fiscal interest for many companies not to report cyber attacks on their networks. In drafting legislation, can any confidentiality safeguards be implemented that would encourage more companies to come forward when they have fallen victim to cyber attacks?

Answer. The Department of Homeland Security (DHS) has a long history of responding to cyber and physical security incidents involving critical infrastructure and protecting the confidentiality of sensitive information through the Protected Critical Infrastructure Information program (PCII). PCII is an information-protection program that enhances voluntary information sharing between infrastructure owners and operators and the Government. If the information submitted satisfies the requirements of the Critical Infrastructure Information Act of 2002, it is protected from disclosure under the Freedom of Information Act; State, Tribal, and local disclosure laws; use in regulatory actions; and use in civil litigation. PCII can only be accessed in accordance with strict safeguarding and handling requirements. Only trained and certified Federal, State, and local government employees or contractors may access PCII.

Designating information as PCII also provides a level of protection that facilitates DHS's ability to work directly with the infrastructure owners and operators to identify vulnerabilities, mitigation strategies, and protective measures. Homeland security partners can be confident that sharing their information with the Government will not expose sensitive or proprietary data, while the Government can still benefit from increased information sharing by analyzing and securing critical infrastructure and protected systems, identifying vulnerabilities and developing risk assessments, and enhancing recovery preparedness measures. Furthermore, timely reporting of serious cyber incidents allows for companies, or the Department, to provide mitigation assistance as soon as possible, often limiting the damage that can be caused and potentially saving on remediation costs.

The Executive Order on Improving Critical Infrastructure Cybersecurity also initiates key information sharing improvements by increasing the security clearances provided to critical infrastructure personnel and expanding a program that enables advanced sharing of cyber threat information to assist participating critical infrastructure companies in their cyber protection efforts. While there is bipartisan consensus on the need for additional information-sharing legislation, the administration is focused on ensuring that the text of any such law fully addresses several key objectives. Specifically, information-sharing legislation must:

- Carefully safeguard privacy and civil liberties, including properly defining the type of information that can be shared, the purposes for which such sharing can occur, establishing adequate oversight, and procedures to remove identifying information unrelated to cybersecurity threats;
- Provide targeted liability protections that explicitly authorize legitimate action without creating unintended consequences;
- Leverage all of the Government's cybersecurity capabilities, while preserving the long-standing, respective roles and missions of civilian and intelligence agencies; and
- Clarify the type of assistance that DHS can provide to quickly help a private-sector company, State, or local government when that organization asks for its help.

QUESTION FROM HONORABLE SUSAN W. BROOKS FOR GARY W. HAYES

Question. In February, the Emergency Alert System of two television stations in Montana was compromised and a fake emergency alert message warning of a zombie apocalypse occurring in several counties. While this incident did not cause any harm, my concern is that the American people rely on public information during crisis and disasters to help guide their actions and hacking into the system could cause great harm or confusion. What are some measures that can be taken to prevent this from occurring again and assure the American people the information we provide through the emergency alert system is accurate?

Answer. Response was not received at the time of publication.

○